Promised Land

Youth Culture, Disruptive Startups, and the Social Music Revolution

KYLE BYLIN

ISBN: 1500598496
ISBN 13: 9781500598495

TABLE OF CONTENTS

The most interesting thing about this book is that it's written by a North Dakota kid who dreamed of being a songwriter and used his writing skills to break into the music business. The irony is that I failed out of College English at Mayville State University because I never read the class-assigned book, *One Day in the Life of Ivan Denisovich*, which I learned counted as a large percentage of your grade. I still remember asking the teacher in the middle of the final exam what the word "emboldened" meant, her telling me that I would know if I had read through the book, and realizing that I was screwed, as there was no way that I would pass.

You wouldn't think that a small town, farm boy would form deep insights into the state of the music business, but thanks in large part to my tech-savvy father I had dial-up Internet and file-sharing clients like everyone else. I still remember using AudioGalaxy to download 10 to 12 songs a night and burning them on to CD for my Walkman. I also remember being a one and a half hour drive from the nearest big box retailer, such as Best Buy or Walmart, and my family only made that trip every few months. I downloaded songs in my teenage days because albums were geographically unavailable and my desktop computer was right in front of me.

If you fast forward about thirteen years later, it still takes the same time to reach Grand Forks, North Dakota and my childhood home looks roughly the same. But I'm a young adult now, this MacBook Air can fit inside a manila envelope, and a mobile app on my iPhone 5 called Spotify is playing "The Messenger" by Linkin Park on repeat. So how did I break into the business? How did we go from illegal access to un-limited music via AudioGalaxy and dial-up to legal access to millions of songs via a smartphone, mobile data, and a streaming service? How did I just share a lyric snippet from this song to all of my friends via Facebook and Twitter?

Well, that is what this collection of essays covers: my journey into the center of the music industry from August 2008 to July 2014. I started writing at 20-years-old as a college student, Target employee, and record label intern. I went on to become the editor of *Hypebot.com*, a chart manager at *Billboard*, and a technology analyst and user researcher at Live Nation Labs, a web and mobile product group inside of the parent company. The first half of the book was mostly written while I worked at Target and *Hypebot.com* in Fargo, North Dakota. The second half was drafted while I held roles at *Billboard* and Live Nation Labs in Los Angeles, California.

During this time, I reported on developments in youth culture and disruptive startups that came together to create major shifts in the music industry. When I joined the online discussion, it centered on the impact of file-sharing clients and whether music fans would purchase digital downloads. People criticized record labels for stonewalling startups and suing fans. As time passed, the conversation shifted toward the rise of smartphones and apps. Music streaming services gained the connectivity and portability needed to interest fans and reach the mainstream market; everyone grew excited about the future of music listening and discovery.

It's interesting to wonder how my 13-year-old self, who grew up in the digital music revolution and used to download songs, would respond if his 26-year-old self traveled back in time and gave him an iPhone 5, complete with mobile data and Spotify's app. He would probably be pissed off that he hasn't (yet) become a famous songwriter, but I think he would be pretty damn excited to learn that he could play whatever song he wanted, wherever he wanted. Given that I can only know my 26-year-old self, who has been using Spotify's app since it launched in the U.S. three years ago, I know that I take unlimited access to music for granted.

But unlimited access to music is the promised land — the musical utopia that my 13-year-old self believed should exist, but took over a decade to develop. We can now play any song that we want on Spotify, follow close friends to see what they are listening to, and share new favorites through the "Messages" feature. We can now hear a song in a coffee shop, identify it using a music-ID app like Shazam or SoundHound, and listen to it through Spotify's app. We can even add the song to our music library, create a radio station, or read the lyrics. Sure, it's still the early days for these music companies, but they are quickly revolutionizing modern life.

INTRODUCTION

Bruce found me in August 2008. I was a 20-year-old college student and an intern at an indie record label in Minneapolis, Minnesota. I had just published my second blog post ever. My readership was small, which is a polite way of saying that the blog I wrote for was viewed only by the other ten people who worked at the label. Though the sequence of events is fuzzy now, I remember the publicist, smiling brightly as always, walking over to the intern cubicle to tell me that a "Bruce Houghton" had contacted her and asked for permission to republish my post on his blog, *Hypebot.com.*

I was floored. I had heard of *Hypebot.com* before, in class. This was a big deal.

Bruce and I exchanged a few emails, and I gave him the okay, and my blog post went up on the site a couple of days later. What happened next neither of us anticipated: Seth Godin, an influential business author and blogger, was the first person to comment on my post. I was ecstatic, and so was Bruce. In the midst of our celebration, Bruce told me that I should send any other ideas for posts his way.

I did just that. Rather than embracing my duties as an intern — solving captcha puzzles and adding friends to the indie bands' MySpace pages — I started sending Bruce new concepts on a regular basis without really knowing what would come of it. I just buried my head in business and psychology books and kept on writing.

By February of 2009, my blog posts were deemed notable enough that Bruce made me an associate editor at *Hypebot.com.* Again, I was astounded. I didn't understand the path I was on or the direction it would take me, but I ran like hell anyway.

Having graduated from college, I decided Minneapolis was not the best place to be during an economic decline, so I moved back home. This was not exactly a logical decision for someone hoping to get a job in the music industry, given that home was a North Dakota farm a few miles outside of Adams, a small-town with a population of 200. There is no "music industry" in North Dakota. I was it.

After a few months, I moved to Fargo, the closest thing to a city in a state with only 650,000 people. The plan: intern in radio to build my resume and hope that would be enough to convince the local concert promoter, a company called Jade Presents, to let me intern for them. My desire to work for the concert promoter was fueled by nostalgia: the rock shows they put on when I was younger were what primed my interest in live music and the music industry.

Unfortunately, radio and I didn't work out. Perhaps, this was because I was more interested in learning about the downfall of commercial radio and its impact on society than I was in operating soundboards and making on-air skits.

I shared my not-so-successful strategy to Bruce one day, and he revealed that he had loose ties to the owner of Jade Presents. He offered to send over some kind words on my behalf. I got an interview with Jade that week, and for the next three months, I became his marketing intern.

Fruition

I worked as an entry-level employee for Target while I hustled in my "free" time. By that, I mean I put in forty hours a week at Target, interned on my days off, and wrote essays for *Hypebot.com* at night. I did sleep — sometimes.

In September 2009, things got even more interesting. I was asked to present at [Next BIG Nashville] in Nashville, Tennessee. The guy who bagged your groceries and helped you locate that one scented candle or picture frame you couldn't find was being asked to present at a music industry conference.

Obviously, I couldn't wear my old red and khaki to the conference. I ran out and bought some fancy clothes. I requested vacation time from Target. The crew from the Next BIG Nashville flew me out to the music capital of the country. I was one step closer to realizing my dream.

I had never done a keynote presentation before, so they decided to interview me on stage instead. My session, "A Conversation with *Hypebot. com's* Kyle Bylin on Digital Natives," was at 3pm on October 7. During the first session, I glanced at the program — and discovered that they had listed me on the front cover. There I was, Kyle Bylin (Target, err, I mean *Hypebot.com*), between Kevin Lyman (Warped Tour) and Steve Robertson (Atlantic Records). The conference was great. Nashville was beautiful. But, as good things often go, my time there ended as quickly as it began.

Back in North Dakota, I resumed work and things went back to normal. During this hectic time, I took constant inspiration from the mantras of entrepreneur Gary Vaynerchuk: "patience and passion" and "stop crying and just keep hustling." In his Web 2.0 Expo talk "Building a Personal Brand Within the Social Media Landscape," Vaynerchuk says that you have to do what you love, and those who truly want to pursue their passions should consider getting jobs in an environment like retail, where you can make just enough money to cover your bills and chase your dreams after hours.

I was passionate about music industry criticism, media ecology, and sociocultural evolution. I wrote my essays after hours, and refused to compromise. My writing was getting better and my ideas only became more extensive. I would finish work in the afternoon around 4:30pm and begin brainstorming and crafting essays and interviews by about 5:30pm, which would continue until past midnight unless I burned out early, and then I'd be up the next morning to do it all over again. I had Thursdays and every other weekend off. I wrote through those, too.

In October 2009, I wrote a *Hypebot.com* post called "Minds for the Future: Why Digital Immersion Matters." Inspired by the book *Born Digital: Understanding the First Generation of Digital Natives*, I reached out to its authors, John Palfrey and Urs Gasser, thinking the post might be of interest to them. They graciously thanked me for sending my essay over and decided it was even worth republishing on the blog they had set up for Harvard Law's Digital Native Project. The essay's appearance there was marked by a few tweets that said some very pleasant things: "Digital Natives project nails it" and "Insightful Harvard blog post."

All this good news made me want to share my successes with the guests who came through my register at Target. You'd be surprised the looks and comments I'd get when I started telling someone buying some Tide that I'm a writer for an influential music industry blog in my spare time, that I've been flown to Nashville to be interviewed at a major industry conference, and that Harvard Law was asking me to contribute to their blog.

"Yeah, right."

Each day that I worked at Target reminded me that I could settle for an average job at an average retailer, but I wanted to do something more remarkable. I was curious. "Curious is the key word," says Seth Godin, "It has nothing to do with income, nothing to do with education. It has to do with a desire to understand, a desire to try, and a desire to push whatever envelope you're interested in." My writing was my envelope.

He continues, "Once recognized, the quiet yet persistent voice of curiosity doesn't go away. Ever. Perhaps such curiosity will hurt until we come to understand the beauty of a journey that might never arrive at an absolute answer. And perhaps it's such curiosity that will lead us to distinguish our own greatness from the mediocrity that stares us in the face."

Where I come from, when people ask what you want to be when you grow up, they're expecting to hear an engineer, an electrician, a nurse, or maybe even a teacher. People don't talk about being part of the music industry. By the time I graduated from high school, I knew that was what I wanted. I even went so far as to pick the most obscure and most impossible job to define — one that didn't even really exist. My dream was to become a cultural critic, research analyst, and thinker in the music industry. Do me a favor: go home and tell your parents — with a straight face — that after they've spent thousands of dollars sending you to college, you want to get a job that you basically made up. If my parents are any indication, it won't go well.

The Dream

In March of 2009, Bruce and I began talking about how we could start working together more; it was a matter of timing. News came that Berklee Online would be offering a course called "Online Music Marketing with Topspin," and we decided that I would take it as a prerequisite to our further involvement. As the enrollment date for the class inched closer, I became more excited. Then, the class got pushed back and instead of taking it in August, I had to wait until January. This was a small setback, but it actually turned out to be a pretty good thing. I buried myself in my work and ended up writing some my best essays during this time.

Once I had completed the class, Bruce began to position me for a start date to work full-time at *Hypebot.com*. I was on my way, not only to getting a job in the music industry, but to getting one I had created.

What did it take to get here? 23 months. 72 books. 100 pieces of content contributed to *Hypebot.com*, many of them essays several thousand words long. I committed myself to keep publishing and pursuing bigger questions, even though they may never have any absolute answers. All it took was time and stepping away from the many distractions of my everyday life. That's what it took for me to go from college student trying to keep busy at a record label internship to full-time editor of *Hypebot.com*.

When I started with Bruce in 2008, he gave me a special opportunity and I had the presence of mind to seize it. Luckily, I had come of age at a time when all of this was possible, when a kid from small town North Dakota could dream of making a living writing about culture, technology, and the music industry, and the tools needed to do that were already in place.

Author Dan Pink argues that the three essential elements to drive — what it takes to truly motivate us — are autonomy, mastery, and purpose. Bruce offered me all three of these things. He gave me the ability to direct my own path and choose the topics I would write about, he helped fuel my desire to get better and better at something that mattered to me, and he let me be a part of *Hypebot.com* — something bigger than myself.

If you are looking for a job in the music industry, or any industry, for that matter, I will say this: you better want this more than you've ever wanted anything in your life. You must be willing to make sacrifices, to put in the hours it takes to make your dreams a reality. My biggest lesson of all: if you want to see the bigger picture, you have to paint it yourself.

June 15, 2010

MARKETING AND MUSIC: FROM POP TARTS TO POP ARTISTS

When marketer Seth Godin talks, people listen. In his book *Purple Cow*, he argues that TV (and stuff like TV) is at the heart of spreading ideas. He explains how major media and retail corporations figured out how to spread their ideas within the system that he calls the "TV-Industrial Complex." They bought ads, which got them more distribution, in turn, allowing them to make bigger profits. Finally, they were able to complete the cycle by using that money to buy more ads.

He goes on to say that companies used this complex to reach people in an unexpected way, a way they didn't necessarily want, by running an ad over and over again until they bought the advertised product. But over the last couple of years, the marketers who brought us the likes of Fruity Pebbles and Pop Tarts have found that these old ways are no longer working.

Record labels used a similar system, but added a few steps.

1) Debut the single three months before the album release; 2) Pay mass radio to play song, three times an hour; 3) Half a month before the album release, send video to MTV and Fuse; 4) Release album on a Tuesday; 5) Rise up the *Billboard* charts; 6) Use profits to buy more

distribution and tour support; 7) Debut the second single two months after the album release; 8) Pay mass radio to play song, three times an hour; 9) Top the *Billboard* at #1; 10) Make second video; 11) Start tour of the United States; 12) Halfway through, release third single; 13) Make third video; 14) Finish the tour; 15) Artist uses whatever money the label didn't take to go on three-year journey, find inner self, and get to work on second album; and 16) Go back to step 1 and repeat.

Like the TV marketers before them, eventually the record labels found that this "CD-Release Complex" stopped working. They spent their money, but the bands they threw at pop radio no longer stuck. No one cared about what they had to say. In a world where people now had many more listening choices and far less time, the obvious thing happened: people started ignoring the efforts of the record labels.

In the YouTube video "An Anthropological Introduction to YouTube," Professor Michael Wesch describes a cultural inversion where the more individualistic people become, the more they both value individualism and desire community. In other words, we become more independent, yet we long for stronger relationships. There is commercialization all around us, therefore, we seek authenticity.

This cultural inversion perfectly describes the way people interact with music now. Many of us have developed very diverse and complex listening habits. We have a strong desire for music that is real, authentic, and meaningful, and we now form communities around our favorite bands, desiring connection and relationship alongside the music we prefer.

As music fans, we are now walking through a crowded marketplace where everyone wants our attention. What happens naturally is that we tune out the noise around us. We construct virtual walls around ourselves that can be permeated only by certain messages. Marketers now have to be smarter about what they do because it's hard to buy their way into our headphones.

As a musician, what relationships are you building? Where is your community? What connections are being made? How authentic is your message?

September 12, 2008

KILLING ITSELF TO LIVE: HOW THE RECORD INDUSTRY CONCEIVED ITS OWN DEMISE

The values of our throwaway culture, where popular products and ideas have a short shelf-life and are quickly discarded for new ones, have now also permeated our relationship with music. This phenomenon plays out when listeners download quickly popularized songs and listen to them repeatedly. Once a song starts to fade into obscurity or has grown tiresome due to loss of novelty, over-exposure, or a "change of taste," the user deletes it from the computer or iPod.

This can be attributed to file-sharing, which changed music fans' relationship with the culture that they consume and the paradoxes of choice they encounter within the Internet realm. More importantly, file-sharing has allowed fans to simulate the decision to buy a song without actually committing themselves financially. This, in turn, has caused them to become increasingly passive about deleting it later on.

Up to this point, why things become unpopular and what affect adoption speed has on the abandonment of cultural tastes has largely remained a mystery. Through their research of over 100 years of data on first-name adoption trends, Jonah Berger from the University of

Pennsylvania and Gael Le Mens from Stanford University and Pompeu Fabra University in Barcelona, found that tastes that quickly increase in popularity die out faster than ones that build more gradually.

More interesting still, these researchers also noted that similar outcomes have been observed in the record industry, where artists who shoot to the top of the charts may be perceived negatively and realize overall lower sales than those who've made a more gradual climb. Simply put, people may avoid buying music from an artist that they consider short-lived because the attractiveness of the music decreases and loses its uniqueness.

"This seemingly counterintuitive finding," they write, "has important implications. It suggests that faster adoption is not only linked to faster death but may also hurt overall success." When we view these findings in light of the ten years preceding and following the rise of Napster and file-sharing, the big picture becomes clearer, adding new insight into how the record industry crashed in the digital age.

Music as a Unit

During the CD boom, which lasted from 1984 to 2000, commercial music became increasingly pressured and scrutinized by executives who demanded that it yield the returns expected of any other business unit. This mindset became one of many catalysts that caused the record industry leadership to change from the savvy executives who nurtured talent and developed careers to the corporate types who relied primarily on the infrastructure established through MTV, big-box retail, and commercial radio.

Greg Kot argues in *Ripped* that, by the late 1990s, the acts dominating the charts were more marketing triumphs than creative ones. And, with the numerous successes of acts like Britney Spears, 'N Sync, the Backstreet Boys, and Ricky Martin, the major labels began to abandon their long-range, career-building strategy of organic growth in favor of the mass-mediated commercial music that could provide stronger quarterly growth and profits.

However, what the hit-factories couldn't create was loyalty. Their practices would come to cast a divide between themselves and a wired generation of fans far more subtle and sophisticated than they ever imagined. Every time the labels used commercial radio and MTV to spike an artist's popularity, they risked, as Berger and Le Mens noted, realizing lower overall sales, because fans would avoid investing in an artist they perceived to be a fad.

Consequentially, once the teen pop bubble burst in 2001 and the performers supporting the record industry could no longer sustain their success, the labels began to wake up to the harsh realities that file-sharing seemingly induced. But no one could have foreseen the vicious cycle that would be created as a result of their drastic misconceptions, or how the convoluted system they spent years supporting would spiral out of control.

The mass-marketing practices that the record industry adopted and mastered in correlation with file-sharing's rise may have created the ultimate paradox. The more the major labels focused on producing music that could be highly and quickly popularized, the more the fans perceived these artists negatively and avoided buying their albums, preferring to file-share their potentially "short-lived" songs instead.

Instant Gratification

The more the music fans file-shared, the more the major labels were forced to produce lowest-common-denominator music, which fed an ever-more vicious cycle. With every new release, and every hot new artist that they used their marketing muscle to spike in popularity, the record industry was killing itself to live. The new breed of music executives were achieving sustainability and profits in the only way they knew how. There was simply no turning back.

The modern record industry relied on the CD-Release Complex, which is based on the premise that fans discover music through the same mediums that major labels use to promote new music. This approach had become so ingrained into the very fabric of their business that, without it, they were lost. Still, they were blind to the fact that the abstract system they had created to commercialize culture and bring music to the masses had now become their mental prison.

Previously, artists were established through word of mouth and constant touring, which gradually built a following and enabled artists to develop their creativity and hone their craft. Yet, every year for the last twenty years, the allotted timetable for an artist to be deemed successful has shortened and expectations have heightened. With the advent of file-sharing and the advances in the Internet, the window of opportunity has shrunk considerably — to almost nothing.

In fact, digital culture has proved to be as unforgiving as the media landscape that preceded it. Due to the instantaneous nature of the Internet and its ability to amplify word of mouth, the growth curve for an artist has compressed from a few years to a few weeks. "Now," as Jordan Kurland, manager of Death Cab for Cutie and Feist, commented in *Ripped*, "you run into this phenomenon with people propping things up that shouldn't be propped up quite so soon." He goes on, "It is a society of instant gratification now, and bands are built up and torn down before they've had a chance to create a body of work that represents who they are or what they can do."

In other words, what we're seeing across the spectrum of the record industry, from the top-down corporate media of major labels to bottom-up participatory culture of the Internet, is that artists who quickly increase in popularity die faster. And, within a climate that supports disposability, the file-sharing community will continue to thrive and feed on the throwaway culture that it has helped to create.

June 23, 2009

INTERCHANGEABLE IDENTITIES: THE COLLISION OF CULTURE, TECHNOLOGY, AND SELF

For those who came of age just before the rise and fall of Napster, the music they listened to depended greatly on the "tyranny of geography." Such tyranny, Chris Anderson suggests in *The Long Tail*, made it so fans had access to purchase the music that existed on the limited shelf space in stores that were within a few miles of their homes. Music listening influences like friends, family, and media remain, but with one exception. "Now," Seth Godin writes in *Tribes*, "the Internet eliminates geography." Looking back, what we have are those who were born digital and the epidemic of file-sharing that preceded them. An entirely different portrait of music consumption has emerged because fans are no longer limited by geography, but only by their ability to imagine and their willingness to explore the abundance of music that lives online.

Many would argue, and correctly so, that the appeal of file-sharing among college students and teenagers is because it made music free. "People often don't care as much about things they don't pay for, and as a result they don't think as much about how they consume them," Anderson says in *Free*, his follow-up release to *The Long Tail*. "Free can encourage gluttony, hoarding, thoughtless consumption, waste, guilt, and greed," he says. He continues that people begin to take stuff because it's there, not necessarily because they want it. Common rhetoric in the record industry still says every song downloaded off the file-sharing networks is a lost sale, which, as Anderson suggests, may not be the case after all.

The problem with the assumption by the record industry is that it negates the core appeal of the Internet. Beyond the information highway's shear capacity for establishing and maintaining connections, it also gives college students and teenagers the ability to experiment, explore, and reinvent their identities. "Digital Natives are certainly experimenting with multiple identities," professors John Palfrey and Urs Gasser write in *Born Digital*. "Sometimes, they are recreating or amplifying aspects of their real-space identities when they go online. In other instances, they are experimenting online with who they are, trying on roles and looks and relationships that they might never dare to try on in real space." It is this aspect of identity experimentation that aligns with file-sharing in the way that college students and teenagers oftentimes will download music that they may have never otherwise considered listening to or buying.

"During our teenage years, we begin to discover that there exists a world of different ideas, different cultures, different people," neurologist Daniel Levitin writes in *This Is Your Brain on Music*. "We experiment with the idea that we don't have to limit our life's course, our personalities, or our decisions to what we were taught by our parents, or to the way we were brought up. We also seek out different kinds of music." This is where the true appeal of file-sharing becomes clear. In the college dorms and bedrooms of Middle America, you have students and teenagers who have questionable access to "good music" via traditional means. Yet, on the Internet lives an abundance of songs that is otherwise inaccessible even with the purchasing power of those teens and their parents combined.

The moment music became digital and shareable on the Internet, everything changed. You had students and teenagers who were essentially consuming and deleting music. They would download seven albums, put them on their iPod, and listen to them for a week. Then they'd delete the four that they didn't like as much and keep the three that they did. All of a sudden, they were less likely to accept sunk costs, which in music is like the following a scenario.

You get so excited for an album that you buy it the day that it comes out. You play the CD. The longer you waited to hear it, the more you'll listen to it. Even if you didn't like it very much, that's okay because maybe it will grow on you. Eventually you stop listening to the album. You could re-sell it, but you probably won't.

Inevitably, with digital music there is a feeling of loss if we purchase an album that didn't live up to our expectations because there is absolutely no resale value. Even if and when we decided to face up to our poor decision and accept the sunk costs, there's no chance to get even a fraction of our money back through resale. College students and teenagers don't have the money for that, especially when they are at a point in their lives where they are experimenting with their identities and their taste in music. We think of file-sharing like stealing, yet no one has taken the time to stop and wonder whether or not the true appeal of file-sharing aligns instead with one's path through adolescence. This is not to be taken as an excuse for behavior that runs contrary to the profitability of an industry, but as a plea for us to reconsider our opinions.

It was the record industry that released their golden compact disc into the hands of college students and teenagers who would later figure out, with the advent of personal burning software, that they could make perfect physical and digital copies of them. Neither the record industry nor the students and teenagers intended to bring a \$15 billion-a-year juggernaut to its knees, but together, they did. Steven Levitt, co-author of *Freakonomics*, says that, "Even when you have someone clever designing the rules, the incentives, with thousands or millions of people with something at stake, scheming on the other side, they almost always figure a way around whatever system you set up." He says, "The most powerful idea of [that law] is that anyone who thinks they can set up a set of rules, thinks they are smarter than the market, in some sense, usually loses." The point being that, for as long as we try to prop up the old model, we are only denying the kind of access to music that the next generation of music fans actually want. They want, to the best of our knowledge, the ability to experiment, explore, and reinvent their tastes in music, much in the same way they do with their identities on social networks. This freedom to be themselves, that's what they really want.

As digital music migrates from iPods to mobile phones, it is necessary to take into account what makes this shift so profound. According to sociologist Barry Wellman, "Computer-supported communication is everywhere, but it is situated nowhere. It is I-alone that is reachable wherever I am: at a home, hotel, office, highway, or shopping center." He says, "The person has become the portal." In recent years, the mobile phone has become not only a fashion object and signifier of social status, but it "has become one dimension of how we construct our own identity." It's the central hub where college students and teenagers navigate their on and offline identities, store their music collections and stay constantly connected to their various worlds. It's their life, in their pocket.

Never before has so much of young peoples' lives been open to interpretation and discrimination. Whether they are conscious of it or not, many of them are making clear public statements about who they are and how they want to be perceived. "The mobile phone is not just a functional item; it is also a symbolic item," Jonathan Donner and Richard Ling write in *Mobile Communication*. "The selection of mobile phones and mobile telephone services is not only a signal to others of how we wish to be seen, but also a way that we integrate our self-image." The identity claims that individuals make with mobile phones are not unlike the ones they make with music. A study called "You Are What You Listen To" found that young people use music "as a badge to convey information about themselves and the social groups to which they belong."

The ownership of the correct type of smartphone, the possession of the right popular songs, and participation on the new social networking site show college students and teenagers are aware of the current fashion and that they actively curate and maintain their own identities. For those who are too passive in this practice, the social consequences are high — they risk being teased and made fun of by their peers for having an older phone or unpopular model. When viewed through the lens of fashion, it becomes clear that the mobile phone and digital music have gone beyond simply being digital technologies and cultural works to being a type of idol in people's pursuit of their own identity.

In *The Tipping Point*, Malcolm Gladwell tells a parable of the epidemic of teen smoking in America that occurred in the 1990s. The arc of his parable applies well to file-sharing. What he observed about smoking at the time is that many of the efforts to stop smoking among teenagers had failed. Measures were taken to restrict and police cigarette advertising, the price of cigarettes was raised, and extensive public health campaigns through various media outlets were run to try educate teens about the dangers of smoking. But still they smoked, and in increasing numbers. "As any parent of a teenage child will tell you," he says, "the essential contrariness of adolescents suggests that the more adults inveigh against smoking and its dangers, the more teens, paradoxically, will want to try it." Sure enough, he argues, that's exactly what happened.

What do the chances of getting cancer later in life have in common with the possibility of being sued for $150,000 per willful infringement of a downloaded track? Well, in a study done in 2006 by Cornell University, researchers concluded that teens are more likely to ponder the risks, take longer in weighing the pros and cons of engaging in high-risk behavior than adults, and actually overestimate the risks. The primary difference between adult and teen risky behavior they found is that in these scenarios teenagers just often decide the benefits outweigh the risks.

Thus far, the record industry has focused on shutting down the services and sites that facilitate file-sharing. It even went as far as targeting and suing individuals in relation to file-sharing. "Which misses the point entirely," Mark Earls, author of *Herd*, argues, "because we are not discrete, self-determining individuals; we do what we do largely because of our interaction with — and under the influence of — others." College students and teenagers share files because everyone else is file-sharing. Almost everyone at their age does it because they too are experimenting with their identities.

Perhaps it isn't a mystery why file-sharing and streaming services like Grooveshark and Rhapsody appeal so deeply to college students and teenagers. At a time of continuous flux in their lives, music becomes their only constant. Given that individuals use music as a vehicle of self-expression, in a world where they are experimenting, exploring, and reinventing their identities, it should be no surprise that they figured out a way around the set of rules. From the point of view of the digital generation, the rules that the record industry put in place in the physical world no longer make any sense in the digital world. Instead of acknowledging the nature of the next generation of consumers, the record industry has simply tried to deny college students and teenagers access to a system that actually appeals to who they are and how they experiment with their identities. In the words of Gladwell: "What we should be doing instead of fighting experimentation is making sure that experimentation doesn't have serious consequences."

November 23, 2009

THE LANGUAGE OF TRIBES: TRUE FANS AND OUTSIDERS

A black concert tour T-shirt became a ubiquitous means for teenagers to advertise that they had personally attended The Who concert in 1974 or Led Zeppelin in 1975. Initially, music fans wore concert T-shirts like a badge proclaiming where they had been and the experiences they had shared. But as concert T-shirts became an essential component of music culture and began to represent the bands themselves, young people wore them to convey information about who the wearers were and the tribes to which they belonged. As a way of externalizing their bond, it wasn't uncommon for members of the same tribes to dress alike. For them, as neurologist Daniel Levitin writes in *This Is Your Brain on Music*, music became "a mark of personal and group identity and of distinction."

Groups such as The Who and Led Zeppelin gave their fans something bigger than themselves to believe in. When musicians are able to create a band that accomplishes this feat, they also create groups of people who feel like they belong — like they are part of a tribe. "People must belong to a tribe; they yearn to have a purpose larger than themselves," E. O. Wilson argued in *Consilience: The Unity of Knowledge*. Wilson went on to say, "We are obliged by the deepest drives of the human spirit to make ourselves more than animated dust, and we must have a story to tell about where we came from and why we are here." Through music, we come to understand ourselves and our place in the world. Music gives us a window into other people's lives. It shows us we are not alone. It tells us that someone else feels like we do.

For a brief moment, the connection that occurs bridges the gap between an artist's creative vision and his or her audience's emotions. It's perhaps the single most important aspect of music. It is in that instant that a song becomes more than a song — it becomes a part of people's lives, their story. How the audience interprets its meaning, makes it their own, and feels that little bit of something awaken deep inside of them is what matters most.

The notion of a "personal relationship" with an artist — that is, an individual's unique interpretation of what an artist's music and lyrics mean — causes discord among people who are fans of the same artists. The difference of opinion that occurs among members of the same tribe is what characterizes what type of a fan they are, how passionate they are about the music, and the depth of involvement in the artist they have. In *Tribes: We Need You to Lead Us*, marketer Seth Godin argues, "Tribes are about faith — about belief in an idea and in a community." He believes that "they are grounded in respect and admiration for the leader of the tribe and for the other members as well."

But do members of the same tribe fully respect each other? Or are there ways in which certain members experience discrimination? In the music domain, there are hierarchies of fans. There are "true fans" and lesser "casual fans." Through speaking in the language of their tribe, members clarify who belongs and who is an outsider.

True Fandom

True fans, as it turns out, don't get along very well. They insist upon comparing and contrasting their knowledge, level of commitment, and point of entry into an artist's career. They put each other under the microscope to see who will be the first to squirm. Fans dissect, pry, and scrutinize each other, all in the hopes of concluding that it is they who are the true fans — that they hold the deepest passion. Only after much discussion and excessive testing will they accept that someone is a part of their tribe — that another truly loves an artist the way they do. No one can fool a true fan. True fans know a language only they can speak fluently — that only a member of their tribe could hope to understand.

It is through this painstaking process of speaking their tribe's native language and of asking questions that only other true fans would know how to answer that true fans seek to differentiate themselves from lesser fans. True fans can then declare their superiority. If a self-proclaimed true fan of an artist can't speak this language, he or she is the lesser fan. If people declare themselves true fans of AFI and *Sing the Sorrow* is their favorite album, but they can't sing the words to "I Wanna Mohawk (But Mom Won't Let Me Get One)" and haven't fallen in love with *The Art of Drowning*, they will be discriminated against by true fans and demoted to the rank of a lowly, lesser fan. And if the entire language seems completely foreign and trivial to someone, that person is clearly an outsider.

However, not all true fans are created equal. Fandom is composed of extremely rigid, yet somewhat permeable, hierarchies. For instance, there are progressives and purists, curious fans and fundamentalists. In the case of Green Day, you'd be considered a purist if you became a true fan of the group during its early years, if *Dookie* and *Insomniac* are your favorite albums and, at first, you even resisted *Nimrod* because you didn't think that punk bands should play acoustic songs such as "Good Riddance (Time of Your Life)," and you hated the new fans the song attracted. Another separating point in Green Day's career came when *American Idiot* was released, when many of the true fans refused to accept the new sound and stopped listening to entirely because the band was different now.

In contrast, progressives are the true fans who continue to grow with artists, throughout their careers, despite newfound commercial appeal or drastic changes in sound. This is what separates curious fans from the fundamentalists. If you are a true fan of Metallica and refuse to acknowledge or even listen to any album that came after … *And Justice for All*, you are a pure fundamentalist. You considered whether The Black Album was acceptable to your faith before you explored it and likely determined that it didn't align with your beliefs. But, if you're a curious progressive, you embraced the tension between your religion and the group's new sound, wrestled with it and through it, and then decided whether to embrace the new album or reject it — to continue being a true fan or not.

Interestingly enough, some true fans opt to stop supporting artists once they've achieved any degree of commercial success. The fans believe that once major labels find an artist who true music fans perceive to be cool and have become devoted to, the labels take those artists, tweak them, and make them more acceptable. And that's when the mass consumer discovers this artist, runs with that group, and then kills it. Portions of the group's core following, of its true fans, will then decide to abandon it. They aren't willing to accept the sacrifices and compromises that must be made if an artist wants to create music with wide appeal but that is no longer "perfect." This is why some true fans hoard artists and refuse to share the music with their friends. These fans fear that success will change those artists and not for the better.

Perhaps no division is more pronounced than is the one that occurs when an artist who had been underground for many years finally gains mainstream traction and appeal. Nothing makes the blood of true fans boil more than does the idea that newcomers enjoy an artist simply because they heard a single on the radio or saw a music video on Fuse. This hatred for these lesser fans is fueled by the belief that they only like the artist because they are popular now and that they don't actually know about any of the group's earlier great work. Mainstream rock fans who have only recently discovered the band Skillet due to the success of *Awake* and appeal of the song "Monster" are likely to experience disdain from true fans who've known Skillet for at least five years.

Sacred Words

Sometimes, as in the case of Linkin Park, the separation between true and lesser fans is not terribly clear because it broke into the mainstream with its debut album *Hybrid Theory* and never had an underground following. But the one-year window between the release of the single "One Step Closer" and the huge success that "In the End" had was just enough to give true fans the ability to fight over who discovered the group first and how all the lesser fans were merely posers. In this respect, when fans of Linkin Park meet, they talk about why the live acoustic version of the song "The Morning After" done in 2001 is better than the collaboration that Chester Bennington did with Julien-K.

True fans know that the live version of "QWERTY" recorded in Tokyo in 2006 is far angrier and passionate than the studio version that was later recorded and released exclusively to the members of the LP Underground. Right? The live version of the song shifted the expectations of what Linkin Park's true fans should anticipate from the release that followed, *Minutes to Midnight.* The fact that the song was actually misleading is what made true fans continue to love the album but still confused as to why the heavier version that emerged didn't relate to the sound that would later emerge. When true fans of Linkin Park talk about these nuances, they create outsiders. This is the gap between those who simply like the band and those who deeply care about how it's progressed.

"If you know the language, you belong," Patrick Hanlon writes in *Primalbranding: Create Zealots for Your Brand, Your Company, and Your Future*. What he argues is that all belief systems include a specialized set of words that must be learned before people can belong to that group espousing them. "The thing about language is that there's always going to be a need for groups to identify themselves apart somehow," says Mark Abley in *Spoken Here: Travels Among Threatened Languages*. He goes on to say, "We live in a society which is incredibly complex and the only way to deal with that is to feel a part of a subgroup or make ourselves an extended family generally, and so one of the really good ways to do that is to baffle outsiders." Tribes use language to help create their culture, but if you take away or change their sacred words, over time, the tribe's sense of identity will slowly erode.

Lesser, more casual fans are what make the songs of the day a part of our collective identity. Even if, in the end, they can't actually speak the language of the tribe, they facilitate the tribe's ability to continue gaining new members. True fans teach outsiders the native language of their tribe, but in the process, outsiders don't share in the joy of discovering and learning about the artist on their own. They were taught. Casual fans are what make the true fan and culture possible. Without them, we would be unable to share our experiences and actually declare ourselves true fans. After all, there's no reason to speak your tribe's native language if no one else understands the words and what makes those words sacred to you.

What's at stake in the digital age in which artists are increasingly catering to their true fans' needs over those of the lesser, more casual fans, is that by adding multiple layers of specialization to the language of their tribe, they minimize the language's potential to be more widely adopted and learned by outsiders. And if these artists' true fans are unwilling to pass on their tribe's native tongue, heritage, and culture or if outsiders simply won't take the time to learn the language, the language itself and the culture it sustains are at risk and could eventually die. If those true fans decide to move on to another artist and quit speaking their native tongue, there will be no new fans to continue the culture the original true fans once created. If a tribe's sense of identity erodes and there's nothing left to believe in then the tribe dies too.

December 21, 2009

THE ELSEWHERE MUSICIAN: MAKING CONNECTIONS IN A FRAGMENTED WORLD

I was ten when I recorded "The Rockafeller Skank" by Fatboy Slim off the radio onto cassette tape. Twelve when the music video "The Real Slim Shady" by Eminem premiered on MTV's Total Request Live. The idea that I could reach out and connect with the artists I liked didn't exist yet or at least wasn't familiar to me. MySpace didn't catch on where I grew up — almost no one that I knew had it. Artists were perceived as unreachable. What you knew about them was based on the lyrics in their songs or maybe a brief interview segment in *Rolling Stone*. Even the concept of sending traditional fan mail was of no interest because there was no expectation that the artist would read or write back. It was the equivalent of trying to send your Christmas list to Santa at the North Pole.

In the truest form, I, along with everyone I knew, were passive consumers of music and thought nothing of tuning into the radio and not getting to choose what songs were playing. Waiting through a few terrible videos on MTV in order to hear something good was commonplace and seen as a way to pass the time. Today, that's no longer the case.

Music fans have set different expectations for artists and insist that they be met. While not everyone has interest in messaging their favorite artist, those that do anticipate a reply. Of course, no one sheds tears when old hats like Metallica or Def Leppard don't reply, but fans of Making April or Owl City have become accustomed to the idea that they can reach out to these artists and make a real connection.

What does this mean for an artist? Think about it as the blurring of the line between the public artist and the private individual at a time when the boundary between home and studio has largely disappeared. On tour, thanks to advances in digital technologies, the ability to stay in touch with their fans has become delocalized for many artists so that it can be done at all hours from almost anywhere. Leisure time once spent doing creative things — when an artist could take time away from it all — has turned into work that ranges from learning how to market oneself online and off, to answering an endless barrage of messages from fans, bloggers, and managers, to trying to keep all of one's profiles, blogs, and social-media tools relevant and up-to-date.

"It's that the once disparate spheres have now collided and interpenetrated each other, creating a sense of 'elsewhere' at all times," writes sociologist Dalton Conley in *Elsewhere, U.S.A.* He continues, "It is the plethora of economic opportunities created by technology that creates a dogging sense of loss, of needing to be elsewhere, doing something different." Whether you equate elsewhere with the next social-networking site that seems to offer more promising opportunities or with the idea that instead of making more music you should be figuring out how to better market the music that you've already made, the message is clear — that what it means to be an artist in the twenty-first century is drastically different from what previous generations have experienced.

Another trend unique to the digital age is the collapse of the creativity timeline. What this refers to is the shrinking amount of time between albums — or any creative output for that matter — based not on the discretion of the artist but on the demands set forth by the changes in society. Prior to this turning point, it wasn't unheard of to let two to three years pass between the time you released and toured an album and the time you started the process of creating and releasing another, which could take another year on top of that. Once completed, a wide variety of radio, print, video, and retail store promotions would be organized by your record label to promote it. Through these mass-media and retail outlets, your fan base would find out about your album and learn when and where they could purchase it.

By today's standards, that mentality of how records ought to be released is suicidal at best. It's not that fans are less loyal than they were before. In fact, the opposite is probably true now that a greater percentage of fans can be more actively involved and invested in an artist's career. It's that with the millions of bands and sheer abundance of music out there, such a lack of immediacy and communication with your fan base would be catastrophic. "For the first time in history, the more we are paid, the more hours we work," Conley writes. "Paradoxically, perhaps, we do this now because among the luckiest of us the rewards for working are so great, they make the 'opportunity cost' of not working all the greater." The result, he argues, is "that we no longer have leisure-class elites."

It used to be that if you worked really hard as an artist and garnered a large-enough following through blood, sweat, and tears — that if you did these things, played enough shows, and were patient enough — a record label might sign you. And, if you were able to consistently make music that people loved and albums that sold millions of copies, you could make music for a living. The remaining, more mundane details and business arrangements would be taken care of by your label, and one day, if you were successful enough, you might actually never have to make music ever again. As counterintuitive as that seems, becoming a top-tier artist meant that you could, in a sense, pursue other interests.

But those dreams have come and gone faster than anyone could have anticipated.

Being a top-tier or middle-class artist in the digital age doesn't mean just working harder or playing more shows than everyone else does. It means working much, much harder. For the music industry no longer holds out the promise for artists that signing to a record label means they will live solely off their musicianship. Artists today can survive doing what they love only as long as they are also willing to don other hats that they may not relish wearing. The impetus, says Conley, lies in the fact that when you start making more money, "the opportunity cost of not working feels greater and the pressure is all the more intense." Not only are you expected to do more with less time — handling both the creative and business aspects of being an artist — but you also have a much smaller window in which to make new music and keep your audience engaged with what you produce.

What we've entered into, according to Scott Kirsner, author of *Fans, Friends and Followers*, is the era of digital creativity. "In this era," he says, "artists have the tools to make anything they can envision, inexpensively . . . They can build teams and collaborate across great distances, bridging divides of language and culture. They can cultivate an audience and communicate with it regularly, carrying it . . . with them from one project to another." This extraordinary opportunity, however, is not without great paradoxes. "Breaking out, somehow, is both more of a possibility than it has ever been — and harder than it has ever been," Kirsner explains. "The attention of an individual audience member anywhere in the world is simultaneously easier to snare . . . and harder than ever to snare."

This era of digital creativity has brought forth the opportunity for what researcher Leisa Reichelt calls "Ambient Intimacy," which she says is "about being able to keep in touch with people with a level of regularity and intimacy that you wouldn't usually have access to, because time and space conspire to make it impossible." Where artists used to be able to define the level of involvement they had in the lives of their fans, they are now left trying to determine how much they're willing to let fans get involved in their own lives. In a social world where, as Conley observes, "modernist distinctions like home–studio, work–leisure, public artist–private individual, and even self–other no longer hold fast," many artists don't know how to draw the line between where fan interaction starts and where it ends.

"Perhaps the most fundamental line that has been breached," Conley argues, "is that between 'self' and 'other.' The interpenetration of the social world into our daily consciousness — our orientation to elsewhere — has the ultimate effect of colonizing and fragmenting not just our attentions but our very identities." He continues, "The result is often a competing cacophony of multiple selves all jostling for pole position in our minds." Somewhere in the middle, artists are caught, perhaps out of necessity, trying their best to navigate this constant stream of communication with their fans — trying to make connections in a fragmented world. All the while wrestling with questions: What if we've revealed too much about ourselves to fans? What if all of the mystery is gone?

Much of this has been made possible in less than a decade. The notion that a middle class of musicians could exist was but a dream not long ago, but with the convergence of the top-down corporate media of major labels and bottom-up participatory culture of the Internet, we are beginning to see these elsewhere musicians and singers emerge. Yet it is only in the last couple years that many of us have begun to wake up to the fact that we can no longer make decisions based on thinking of music as product. Instead, we must begin thinking about music as culture. For the fate of our music culture, now rests not only within the palm of our hands, but within those of future generations as well.

November 12, 2009

THE BARRIERS OF MUSIC
CONSUMPTION: PAST AND PRESENT

There was a time when songs were songs. When there were the albums that you owned and those that you did not. When there was a distinct difference between the music that you liked and the artists that you didn't care for at all.

There was a time when the music that you collected was actually a physical thing. It represented your identity and served as a mirror of your taste. When the albums you had access to, beyond those that you owned, were limited to those of your friends and family. When the only way you could expand your collection was to purchase more music or borrow from someone.

There was a time — one I barely remember — when these boundaries defined my music experience, but those days are gone now, and we can never get them back. Once the album format became fractured and individual songs became the focal point of music consumption, companies like Pandora and Last.FM began the process of discerning the unique characteristics of each song and building recommendation engines around them.

What happened as a consequence of their efforts is that each song transformed into a portal. These "gateways" could be opened up, enabling fans to travel almost effortlessly from one sphere of musical influence to another similar sphere.

Each particular sphere, if traversed, would take one to new spheres of musical influence that existed outside of one's current taste. Thus, individual songs not only became the primary way that fans consumed music, but songs also became a vehicle for music discovery.

Prior to this shift — brought forth by the MP3 format — individual songs only existed within the context of the other songs on the mixtape, radio playlist, or album. Most of the casual fans of an artist never listened to or came into to contact with the other songs on an album since more often than not, the singles were the only songs that existed outside of the album. In the pre-MP3 era, the act of collecting music consisted solely of the ownership of the whole album, of the stack of jewel cases that sat next to your stereo. For fans who wanted to expand their music collections, the only barriers that prevented them from doing so related to the location of the nearest record store and money. Since music was a relatively costly thing to collect on a per-album basis, most people had relatively small collections — in comparison to the more diehard or "true" fans — if indeed they collected any music at all.

Barriers of Music

Then, in the span of about ten years, the proliferation of the personal computer, the shift from dial-up to high-speed Internet, the increased processing power and hard-drive space in computers, the falling cost of blank media and external hard drives, the widespread use of CD burners, the social phenomenon of the iPod and iTunes, and the epidemic of file-sharing occurred. With these societal and technological shifts, the barriers that defined music experiences of previous generations and the act of collecting music fell.

To anyone who had access to and was literate in these digital technologies and services, music became "democratized." The act of collecting music shifted. The limited access that fans had to music and the money they had to buy it was replaced by the amount of time or number of social connections that they had. There were no longer the albums that they owned and those that they did not, but those that they had, those that they aspired to have, and those that they didn't have yet. A song they heard on Pandora five minutes ago was then downloaded onto their computer, listened to, shared with friends over IM, and now — with a few mouse clicks — everyone is listening to that same song. It's a part of multiple collections.

The barriers of music consumption between two friends are gone.

Essentially, with these shifts, anyone who truly wanted to engage in the act of collecting music could. And, in the matter of a month, or even days, they could amass their own collection — one that, by comparison, dwarfed those that previous generations considered substantial.

Soon enough, the process of burning downloaded music onto blank media could be skipped and transferred to an iPod in a matter of minutes. With this barrier removed, file-sharing, as Douglas Rushkoff observes in his book *Life Inc.*, "has been reduced to a frenzy of acquisition that has less to do with music than it does the ever-expanding hard drives of successive iPods." At first, it was a matter of filling an iPod with 2,000 songs, but today it's a matter of acquiring upwards of 40,000 songs on the average iPod.

Fractured Collections

With the barriers to the act of collecting music set so low, another subtle but significant shift occurred: the psychology behind the acquisition of music changed.

In earlier years, music was collected with the notion of longevity in mind, as it best reflected one's taste in music at that moment. In contrast, for those who engaged in the act of acquiring music through other means, like file-sharing, their taste encompassed past, present, and future interests. Their collections reflected not only their inherent taste and disposition toward certain types of music, but that of their peer group and those with whom they surrounded themselves.

Thus, distinct differences between the music that they liked and the artists that they didn't care for at all became increasingly blurred, and so did the contents of their music collections.

In a sense, though, the collections of those who were born digital are not complete. They're fractured, consisting of bits and pieces of everything, of songs divorced from their origins and physical packaging. These songs stand alone — void of everything but the artist's name, the album's title, and the digital cover art. The iPod is merely a container for culture, whereas the jewel case, booklet, and liner notes served to embody culture, to communicate its identity, and to mirror the taste of its owner. An iPod can show the personality of the owner, but says little about the soul of the music.

While it may seem like strangers greet physical music collections and iPods with a similar sense of awe and reverence, it's important to recognize the disparity between the two. The emotions experienced in the presence of unique works of art, and those felt while holding an iPod — which happens to contain art — shouldn't be confused, especially since one relates to the "aura" of the music, and the other to a piece of technology. In the first scenario, when those of previous generations encountered a physical collection, they pored over it, investigated it, held it in their hands — works that weren't their own, but still provoked meaning and were intrinsically tied to their own stories.

Now those who were born digital don't hold the works of art, they embrace the iPod. And when they encounter the collection, while they do still pore over it and investigate it as they scroll through it, that sense of awe and reverence is lost.

The music in the collection is presented devoid of its aura: in the words of Douglas Rushkoff, "It has been removed from its context — from the material processes of its creation." Their emotional experience relates not to being in the presence of unique works of art, but solely to the moment of social connection and identification with the other person. This understated difference — in how works of art are experienced — relates to yet another shift in music culture that separates those who were born digital from those of previous generations.

Internet Is Freedom

For some, these shifts mean the dawning of a whole new era. For others — having come of age during the proliferation of digital technologies, the social epidemic of file-sharing, the explosion in music choices, the splintering of genres into niches, the rise of the personalized music experience, and the increased emphasis on recommendation engines and social filters — this is the reality they've come to know. But for the rest, those who've lived cradle to grave in the digital era, this is the only reality they've ever known. To them, there is no before file-sharing and the Internet — only these societal and technological shifts, and their aftermath.

Those who were born digital don't remember a world in which there were the albums that they owned and those that they did not. The music that they collect isn't a physical thing anymore, it's just files. Sure, those files represent their identity and serve as a mirror of their taste, but they also represent the identities and tastes of everyone that they surround themselves with. Initially, they may have been limited to their friends' and family's collections, but as they became literate in these digital technologies and services, they were only limited by their imaginations, curiosity, and desire to explore.

To them, the Internet is freedom and the record industry won't beat them. The industry can't keep trying to rebuild all of the barriers that defined music experiences of previous generations and the act of collecting music as if, once those barriers were restored, those who were born digital would revert back to "normal." To them, the way in which they consume music is normal.

In the digital era, the record industry has tried to vigorously enforce the barriers to music that defined the experiences of previous generations upon those who were born digital. And, in turn, the newcomers have only resisted ever more destructively. Before we attempt to deny the very nature of the barriers to music in the present by changing them back to the past, we need to recognize that those born digital, those who have immersed themselves in the social ecology of music culture that's forming online, are different now.

To understand why that is, we must first examine the biases of the traditional music delivery system and the specific delivery mechanisms that govern it, then compare them with those of this "other" music delivery system that those born digital have also experienced. Only after we've done this will we be able to come to terms with the truth: that it's not those who were born digital who are "broken."

Rather, it's our traditional music delivery system that's broken. And it's about time that the record industry stops pretending that its barriers still define the way listeners experience music.

April 12, 2010

THE BROKEN SYSTEM: DECONSTRUCTING MUSIC CONSUMPTION

The traditional music delivery system is biased towards hoarding and scarcity. It promoted the gradual development of taste and encouraged the act of collecting music so that each fan could have his or her own access point to the artist's songs. Listening to music independently, in the absence of the artist, means that each individual fan could develop his or her own perspective of the artists and their music. It allows opportunity to scrutinize or discover meaning from the artist in isolation. So, many fans formed intimate, parasocial relationships with the artist where they knew of the emotions of the artist and filled in the rest of the details of the artist's life without the artist knowing theirs. The artist spoke to the fan through their music, but the fan did not "speak" to them.

Through specific delivery outlets — primarily commercial radio, MTV, big-box retail, and print — music was advertised to the fans. These organizations stimulated demand for the music that they promoted over other artists in the marketplace. They established a sense of trust between fans and their corporate-created brand, elevating the artist from performer to idol. This transformation allowed for a common yet commercial music culture to form where fans belonged to something bigger than themselves and socially identified with each other through the relationships that they had with these abstract, top-down artist brands. The act of collecting the artists' music, owning it, and displaying it — this is how fans signaled their preferences, tastes, and identities.

In this delivery system, the artists could disconnect themselves from the fans and create new albums without fear of losing their audience because the taste in music of each fan developed gradually over the course of most of their lives. A new album was to be anticipated, cherished, and hoarded because the artist's creativity timeline lasted several years. In turn, fans viewed the artist's music as a rarity, which is the reason why they waited outside of the store hours before it opened just to purchase the new album.

Biased Mediums

Fans did not have any control over the traditional system. As individual fans — and, by definition, "passive" listeners — they didn't actually know what music they wanted to listen to. Nor did they want to take the time to find it. Therefore, the artist's music had to penetrate the environment of listeners. A single would have to receive heavy rotation on commercial radio, a video would have to be played on MTV, the album would need to be available at all big-box retail outlets, and a review would have to appear in Rolling Stone. When utilized together, these media and retail outlets formed an abstract delivery system that major labels used to influence passive listeners and their taste in music as well as regulate the flow of culture into their lives. This often resulted in a bond between the outlets and the individual that grew stronger than their connection to the actual music that they delivered.

If you focus on these specific outlets and how they distribute commercial culture, it's clear that we are oblivious to the effects of their structural influence. We miss how they promoted the gradual yet subtle development of taste in music over long periods of time.

MTV, print, radio, and big-box retailers are biased toward familiarity and conformity. Even more so, they're biased toward major label interests and the needs of their advertisers.

Commercial radio, for instance, typically cannot play new music. In order to keep the listener's attention for the longest period of time — so that they are exposed to the station's advertisers — they must achieve the lowest tune-out rate possible. And what is required of them to accomplish this feat is that they must maintain the least objectionable programming possible.

When these stations do introduce new music, it can't be radically different from the current playlist — so the comfort of the listener isn't obstructed to the degree that he or she tunes out. The artist's hit single, then, must be familiar to the fan and conform to the rest of the station's programming and that of the current popular music trends. In other words, the music that they play can be new for as long as it offends the fewest people and serves as a buffer between two advertisements.

As for MTV, media critic Douglas Rushkoff writes in his book *Life Inc.* that "They are not dedicated to creating new kinds of music and entertainment in order to promote a richer culture. Corporations depend on understanding trends so they can sell people whatever it is that they already have."

Together, the media and retailers created a focal point in the mindless feedback loop between production and consumption in the traditional system — where industry executives researched teen culture for indications on what music they should play — while teens themselves scoured these mediums for models of new artists to imitate and for the theme songs of their generation.

Taste in Music

Thus, when fans did discover music through these mediums, it is quite likely that their tastes in music would only broaden ever so slightly. And due to the biases of the media and retail outlets, their taste would constantly be reinforced but never challenged; it would evolve along the taste continuum, from one finite state to the next, without dramatically changing.

For the passive teenage listener — whose taste in music was primarily influenced by specific delivery media and retail outlets — the Internet changed all of this.

Prior to the digital revolution, we tended to think of taste as something that goes through a gradual transition from one condition to a different condition — with very few abrupt changes. During our teenage years, interest in music peaks, and we move through the states more rapidly, which carries onward to college — where we were confronted with a multitude of new influences and musical tastes.

After these critical stages in our development, it is understood that this process slows down and, for the most part, that our musical tastes are fully formed. Yet this conventional model of how musical taste develops isn't representative of the personality of each individual fan as much as it is the biases of the consumption systems they interacted with and the ranges of social behavior they promoted.

This raises an important question: if the traditional system facilitated an environment where taste developed gradually, what did the Internet enable?

In short, it permitted a population of digital youth to rethink their role as passive listeners in the traditional system and to become more actively engaged in their culture experiences in a way that wasn't possible a decade ago. First came file-sharing. Then, in an attempt to provide legal services that were more in line with the emerging social norms of those who were born digital, many companies began inhabiting this new landscape. This led to the rise of the personalized music experience and the networked audience.

Finite to Fluidity

Through this social ecology of music culture that formed online, listeners could now exercise a higher degree of control over how they discovered, acquired, consumed, and discarded music. Furthermore, out of this chaos and transformation, an unplanned and unforeseen Internet-era delivery system emerged.

Where the traditional system operated on the assumptions that a fan's taste developed gradually, where collecting music consisted solely of the ownership of physical albums, and where the biases of the delivery system promoted compatible ranges of social behavior, the Internet-era system did not.

In contrasting the traditional music delivery system with that of the Internet-era system that those born digital also experienced, what becomes clear is that it is biased toward different things.

The traditional system and its specific mediums — commercial radio, MTV, big-box retail, and print — are biased toward familiarity, conformity, and facade, and they facilitate the gradual development of taste. On the other hand, the Internet-era system and its equivalent mediums — YouTube, Pandora, iTunes, and blogs — are biased toward personalization, specialization, and relevance. As a result, this new system enables a much more rapid evolution of taste. Therefore, the ranges of social behavior that it promotes are different, too.

As a result, those who were born digital — that is, those who actively engaged with and readily immersed themselves in this Internet-era system — have shifted from finite to fluidity both in terms of how their taste in music develops and how it reflects upon the music they collect. What this means is that their tastes no longer progress gradually along the continuum from one finite state to a different finite state. Instead, they evolve continuously, ultimately reaching a constant state of fluidity.

Also, where the traditional system is biased toward hoarding and scarcity and encouraged the act of collecting music in the physical or finite form, the Internet-era system is biased toward sharing and abundance. It thrives on the collecting of music — across multiple channels — in digital or fluid form.

The Ongoing Redesign

The traditional system is optimized for a different era than the one we are living in today. The Internet-era music delivery system has promoted ranges of social behavior in those who were born digital that are incompatible not only with the traditional system but with the assumptions that the record industry currently operates under.

In the digital age, there will be various systems promoting complex and different ranges of social behavior. If each fan personalizes his or her own delivery system to his or her needs, that person's behavior will no longer align with any one particular system. In a sense, how the individual's taste in music develops and how it reflects upon the music he or she collects will be unique to that specific person.

The traditional system has broken for good. And by treating it as if it still defines how those who were born digital consume music, we are only denying ourselves access to its ongoing redesign.

April 21, 2010

ON FILE-SHARING: ARE YOU SMARTER THAN A 12TH GRADER?

Back in February of 2010, I stumbled across an essay in the written by a twelfth grader named Kamal Dhillon. He argues that file-sharing may be illegal, but is not ethically wrong. The essay had been entered into the Glassen Ethics Competition, and Dhillon won. Out of eighty entrants in the contest who wrote about whether it's okay to download music, movies, and games without paying, the essay that won the $1,000 prize and got republished in the *Winnipeg Free Press* argued that, yes, copyright infringement can be morally justified. Through the views Dhillon expresses, the sheer intellectual resilience that he displays, and his understanding of these complex issues, the essay got me thinking. What happens when fans are not stupid anymore? What happens when the executives and artists who get quoted in the headlines don't have a firm grasp on the file-sharing debate as high school students? I mean, they are smarter than a twelfth grader — right? Most likely not.

Readers of blogs like *Music Think Tank* and *TechDirt*, who live to learn about and make sense of the impact of technology on the recording industry and have observed how file-sharing has reshaped our cultural lives (i.e. you) are smarter than a twelfth grader. But what about those out-of-touch executives, commonly thought of as "struggling dinosaurs," whose only exit from this industry entails mass extinction of their kind and the destruction of the music empires they created? What about all those artists in recent years who have made off-the-cuff comments about file-sharing, only to be criticized for their complete disconnect from the arguments? Better, how do Dhillon's arguments stack up against some of the viewpoints that have been gaining traction?

The other day, audio engineer Jon Sheldrick published his thoughtful post "Why You Should Pay for Music." In it, he argues that rather than "scaring people into buying music," there should be "a culture in which people actually want to spend money on music because they understand the positive repercussions it has on the medium of recorded music, and the lives of the artists that produce it." In contrast, Dhillon believes that society "has benefited overall from file-sharing." He argues that people should become active participants in their cultural lives, but they should also be able to deconstruct the obfuscation in the arguments that surround file-sharing. He is realistic in his observation that millions of people engage in the act of downloading music and find the arguments against it to be "unfair, inconsistent, and irrational." How does Sheldrick fair?

The Value of Music

"The problem," Sheldrick argues, "is that many people just don't value music in a meaningful way." This is the first of many instances where I happen to disagree with Sheldrick. He argues that people value music "in the sense that they enjoy it, and love rocking out on their iPod. However, they don't value it in the sense that they will willingly fork over $1 for a song," enabling the artist to keep producing music. This argument is misguided because it fails to ask the more meaningful question:

Is it that people do not value music, or is it that music has in some way become disconnected from its value?

The answer is that, with the rise of corporatism in the record industry throughout the 1980s and 90s, executives disconnected themselves from what used to matter the most: the music. As the business evolved from the long-term, career-building view that artist development allowed to the short-term, hit-making machine that mass media provided, executives grew dependent on a business scheme that was never intended to serve fans as actual people who had a personal connection to their music culture. Rather, the workings of the CD-Release Complex reduced fans to a mere collective of consumers. They were free to make meaning together — through top-down artist brands and their music — as long as they did so as identity-seeking individuals. The artist "brand" replaced peer-to-peer human relationships with an abstract, corporate-created one, and functioned as the fan's belief system. It employed mythologies, sacred rituals, and iconography that served as a substitute for the features of a real artist. This corporatization continued on to local radio stations and record stores and reduced the natural progression of music culture. It oversimplified the process by which real culture develops and evolves.

Over a few decades, the music culture in which people participated became tilted toward the priorities and behaviors of the multinational corporations and media conglomerates that were responsible for its planning. In the process, our culture became dismantled and replaced with simulations of culture — big-box retail outlets, commercial radio stations, and MTV. As the record industry skewed itself toward corporate needs, it became harder for real culture to thrive. The further people got from the process through which music is created and culture is formed, the more disconnected people became from their value. And the more music culture became detached from its origins and exchanged for a corporate simulation of one — an existence meant solely to promote behavior that improves the profits of the corporations manufacturing it — the more that music became disconnected from its value and the material processes of its creation. By 1999, the height of the record industry, it was a nearly $15 billion a year business. At that point, most people's relationships to the artists they loved were mediated through corporations. Fans grew dependent on artist brands for self-presentation and consumption became participation in their cultural lives — their path to individualism. These paths, however, only further separated and disconnected fans from music culture.

More than a decade later, we still identify with and are even more fascinated by the plight these abstract corporations face in the digital age than we are with the flesh-and-blood artists that they represent. Why do you think that is? Do you really think it is because "people don't value music in a meaningful way"? I would say the argument is more complicated than Sheldrick leads us to believe. Has music become devalued to some degree due to the social epidemic of file-sharing and those born digital who have embraced it? Sure. But, music fans have become disconnected, too.

Misunderstanding Complex Events

Next, Sheldrick shares his experience of what it was like to download music illegally in high school, and then a few years later, as a recording engineer, to witness firsthand the effects that the social epidemic of file-sharing had on the very industry he was attempting to enter. There were artists with sizeable fan bases questioning whether or not they could afford to record another album even though there was obvious demand. There were musicians no longer able to afford to pay recording engineers, and studios, big and small, all over New York City were shutting their doors. All of this, Sheldrick writes, "was a direct result of people not paying for music."

Okay, stop. First off, the problem with Sheldrick's perspective is that he forgets, as a recording engineer, just how vast the chasm is between him and real people. It would be beneficial if more people had experiences like Sheldrick's. Such experiences are illuminating, but it is important to remember that it is real people — not recording engineers — who determine the fate of music culture. The two groups may have the same experiences but see them very differently. The reason for this is that, sure, such experiences would help remind listeners of the significance and value of music. However, in reminding them, we are admitting something important to our understanding of this debate and the shortcomings of Sheldrick's argument. Not only is there an apparent disconnect between listeners and the value of music, but that the inherent value of music has become disconnected from the music itself. Undoubtedly, over the course of the era of recorded music (approximately the last hundred years) people, in becoming more passive participants in their cultural lives, lost their connection to artists and to the labor that creates music. For most people, their participation begins and ends at consumption. They are not as sensitive to the material process of art's creation as Sheldrick, nor do they have a vested interest in maintaining the barriers of music consumption and keeping them as high as possible.

This is why the rift between real people and music industry professionals is so prevalent. Music industry professionals are committed to solving particular problems like financing and distributing recorded music. Therefore, when something like file-sharing comes along and disrupts the process through which those operations occur, and the business model of the record industry, it is important to remember that real people are not committed to preserving the financial hurdles to music consumption in order to keep the record industry's solution viable. And since it is real people, not professionals, who determine the fate of our culture, we must view the Web as an opportunity to reconnect them to the process through which music is made. That way, they have a direct experience of the labor that goes into creating music and not just someone telling them about it.

In addition to this, Sheldrick falls into the cognition trap called "causefusion." In *Blunder*, historian Zachary Shore argues that this trap pertains to "any misunderstanding about the causes of complex events"; it "leads us to oversimplify, often at our own peril." Tell me, Sheldrick, were these things that you witnessed a direct result of file-sharing, or were there other things happening? Beyond the social epidemic of file-sharing, it is more useful to consider things like the rise of the networked audience and the personalized music experience, the death of the CD-Release Complex and the fall of mass marketing, and the fracturing of the media landscape into niches. How about taking the end of the format replacement cycle, the explosion of alternate and immersive entertainment options, and the converging of top-down corporate media with the bottom-up participatory culture of the Internet into consideration. And let's not forget the evolution of social music and the "broken" condition of the traditional music consumption system. Likely, these technological and societal shifts had much more to do with the tragedies that Sheldrick witnessed. File-sharing played a minor role, if any.

After this, Sheldrick changes the topic of his argument and expresses his view on how recorded music "provides a listening experience that is unique and rewarding in its own right, and listeners should strive to preserve that." Is this possible? I mean, can listeners strive to preserve the listening experience? Romantic notions such as this tend to forget that listeners do not program the media through which they hear music. Therefore, the biases of the media that they are susceptible to are also not under their control. Though many audiophiles likely thought about boycotting the widely adopted iPod, the average person's listening habits do change, and they are not precisely "in control" of that. Media is biased; it promotes different ranges of social behavior. If you want to live in the woods with your 45s and listen to them on your record player, do it — but it's hard to say it is up to listeners to preserve the experience. In an ironic twist, Sheldrick follows this logic by making an assertion that aligns directly with thoughts that I have recently been exploring. He argues that fans need to buy their music, learn how to listen more closely and savor it — that by purchasing music and going through the process to obtain it (the waiting, the anticipation, and getting to finally own it), they will inherently enjoy the music more. Exactly. But there's a problem with getting to a place where you can actually savor your music: you have to buy it first. If the arguments I have made about the paradoxes of choice overload in culture are correct, then it is getting harder and harder for fans to decide what music to buy every day and their ability to savor their music is overtaken by the effect of overwhelming choice.

The Morality Issue

"At the end of the day, it's really a moral argument," Sheldrick concludes. However, he concedes that in the music world, much like in life in general, "the moral road is not always the easiest route to take." To understand the limitations of this argument, let us return again to the views Kamal Dhillon expressed in his winning essay. He writes that, "in many areas the world over, the action of uploading and downloading copyrighted material is illegal, and people know this. Yet, they still download music without paying anyway." Why, then, are so many people choosing to simply ignore the copyright laws? "Part of the reason is that people question whether the law that forbids sharing of such material online is morally justified," he answers. On the topic of the morality of file-sharing, he rather convincingly argues that, "The fact that something is illegal doesn't mean that it's necessarily immoral." He argues that, on a global scale, "young people are questioning the merit of the laws that forbid them to share material." They think copyright laws are unjust and know they are easy to break without getting caught. Just as important, Dhillon asserts, is that most young people regard the act of sharing their music with others as morally acceptable.

So, is it really a moral argument? "You're talking about a nonviolent activity largely in the privacy of your own home, or bedroom or dorm room, in search of great music that turns you on — that is inherently a joyful, if potentially addictive, activity," music critic Greg Kot told me in an interview. "It's also completely organic: The Internet, above all, is a tool for sending and receiving files. That music files would be part of that culture is only natural." In *Moral Panics and the Copyright Wars*, legal scholar William Patry argues that the only reason the subject of morality comes up in the file-sharing debates is that people use it "as a way to cover up the inability to justify expansion of rights on economic grounds."

Mike Masnick of *TechDirt* adds to the debate, "Since copyright is intended as an economic right, the argument over copyright needs to focus on the economic issues . . . a properly calibrated system is one where there's the greatest overall economic good and everyone has the greatest opportunity to benefit." At that point, he rightfully asks, "where's the morality question at all?" There isn't one. Those who claim morality in an economics discussion on copyright use it as a crutch because they cannot support their position. Masnick then firmly states, "There is no moral issue at all." In other words, it is not that the moral road is a difficult route to take, as Sheldrick wrote, but that in debating the issue of file-sharing, it is a route that should not be taken at all. Under scrutiny, the argument just does not hold up. Masnick believes that those who use the morality foundation to support their arguments are wrong on two major points. "First," he says, "is the idea that it means creators of content can't make any money" — when in fact, he argues, "nothing can be further from the truth." Then, he argues that the second point revolves around the idea "that there's a right to make money." He maintains his position that this line of logic is completely false because economics is not a moral issue; it does not care about anyone's "right" to make money from his or her creative output. Therefore, neither should you.

Andrew Dubber of *New Music Strategies* has summed up this argument quite well. He writes, "Making music is not (usually) a job of work. It is a creative act. You don't have the RIGHT to make money from your music. You only have the opportunity. If you make music speculatively — that is, you create it in the hopes of making money from it — then you are a music entrepreneur. As such, entrepreneurship rules apply." Even though many artists invest a good deal of energy, effort, and expense in their creative ideas, they will probably make no money. The thing that most people forget is that nobody owes them the money just because they put in the work. To be successful entrepreneurs, artists have to meet people's needs and wants in a way that allows them to make money — not by, as Dubber puts it, "making things that people will not pay for, insisting that they should, and then complaining that their morals are to blame." He then poses this question: "Even if it was true that all the people you wish to target with your art are immoral thieves, why would you insist on trying to change their behavior as part of your business strategy?" After all, Mark Earls wrote an entire book on this topic called *Herd*. Its lesson was, "Mass behavior is hard to change."

To be clear, my intention is not to suggest that Jon Sheldrick is not smarter than a twelfth grader — not at all. He has written a very well thought out essay, and it deserves the attention it has garnered. However, we need to take a moment and recognize the implications of a culture where a twelfth grader is capable of understanding and expressing the arguments that surround file-sharing. When presented with an essay like Sheldrick's, as good as it is, someone like Dhillon is capable of finding his way through the maze of the issues and asking the follow-up question that makes Sheldrick's argument drop like a house of cards. Dillon likely did not know about Masnick, Patry, or Dubber, but the information is out there. Fans are not stupid. Yes, file-sharing is illegal but to them, it is not wrong. Therefore, making these outdated pleas, which are based on arguments that have been debunked by leading experts about why music should be bought is not going to resonate with fans. You tell the right crowd that file-sharing is a moral argument and they are going to think you are an idiot. Not only that, but making file-sharing a moral question does not lead to any imaginative or creative insights. It does not help people understand the issues better. All it does is make artists and employees in the cultural industries feel better about themselves. Instead of taking what could be a great opportunity to clarify the issues that surround this social behavior, and helping the general public comprehend the situation, I would contend that all Sheldrick has done is confused the issues further and turned the discourse into post-lunch student chatter.

July 13, 2010

PARADOX OR PARADISE: MUSIC CHOICE IN THE DIGITAL AGE

There are many reasons to believe that the web has created a "paradise of music" for fans, but that is not necessarily the case. Psychologist Barry Schwartz suspects that a culture plentiful with music has the potential to lessen the amount of satisfaction that fans get from their choices, and increasingly causes them to opt out of the process altogether. In a paper titled "Can There Ever Be Too Many Flowers Blooming?" Schwartz outlines three of the paradoxical effects of choice overload in the cultural domain.

First, when fans are overloaded with cultural alternatives, Schwartz says they will "Opt for the same old thing as a way to avoid facing unlimited options." Similar to the reaction a consumer has to abundance in the material domain, fans will opt for the same old music for a number of reasons. Many fans, out of comfort, do not deviate too far from their favorites. That way they are free from the disappointment they might experience in listening to music that is dissimilar from their established taste. So too, fans tend to have a deep memory of being burned. When purchasing music, they are more prone to remember all the times the music did not work out as opposed to the times it did. Also, fans stick with what they know because there is instant gratification in that music; it never ceases to fit their mood or remind them of when they were growing up. Lastly, fans opt for the familiar because they are genre loyal and often have rigid tastes. In music, this paradox can be readily observed every day. Most passive fans are not interested in new music, unless it is propped up by commercial radio stations or the clubs they frequent. Those of previous generations, especially since most of the new songs out there are not targeted at them anyway, do not want to hear new music nor do they care about it at all. In effect, older fans would rather just listen to the songs that came out when they were younger.

"Think about what 'knowing what you want' means that you are not so open to cultural diversity or serendipity. Instead, you put blinders on, and walk straight ahead until you find what you're looking for." With the explosion of music choice, the splintering of genres into niches, and the fracturing of the album format, making a truly informed selection from this plethora of music becomes difficult if not entirely impossible. Fans might be able to find out about some of the artists, but not all of them. In the place of a considered decision, Schwartz says fans end up falling back on "a variety of labor-saving heuristics which 'solve' the choice problem by making them much more passive decision makers." His fear is that when a fan is overloaded, they will just stay with the same old music and decide that venturing into the cornucopia of music online is not worth their time, since, at least in their minds, they have already done the best they can do.

The Filter Problem

Next, Schwartz argues that when fans are overloaded, they rely on "filters rather than on themselves." Like many fans, I listen to music on Pandora, and while their suggestions as to what I might enjoy listening to are not always perfect, I do value them. In effect, I am using Pandora to be my filter

— my "professional DJ." Pandora will suggest music that is similar to songs I have already heard. Its aim is the opposite of diversity. What Pandora promotes is micro-specialization. It delves deeper and deeper into Miniature Tigers, Anthem of Silence, and Joe Pug — music I already enjoy — in hopes that it will find a more obscure song that is equally satisfying. But, unless I feed Pandora a new station, it will never attempt to broaden my taste with a suggestion to listen to a pop or hip-hop song.

Schwartz believes that the "twin phenomenon" of relying on filters or only purchasing culture you think you want is spreading. He further argues that this is a response "to overwhelming choice in the world of culture." This paradox, along with fans opting for the familiar, may explain why radio remains relatively popular despite the prognostication of the death of radio by media futurists.

Yet, the emergence of many sites and services as answers to this plethora of music online tells us something very important. "Our cultural experiences will only be as diverse as the filters we use to help us select them. With all that is available to us, unmediated browsing is impossible," Schwartz forewarns. "We are more reliant on filters now than we ever were before." To which he adds, "But unless people are deliberate about the filters they use, their own cultural experiences will be anything but diverse." What is more, based upon what we've learned so far about how paralyzing unlimited choice can be, Schwartz's suspicion is that, "in the realm of culture, the more options there are, the more driven most people will be to settle on the most choice-simplifying filters they can find." This is not a good thing. Remember now that it was Chris Anderson in his book *The Long Tail* who made the argument that if this multitude of choice could be organized in a way that was more meaningful, fans would not find it oppressive. It would be less overwhelming. However, what he did not seem to anticipate is that this "rearrangement" of choice could have the effect of making fans even more passive consumers of culture.

Passivity, Not Activity

Third and worse still according to Schwartz's research paper, a consequence of a culture abundant with music is that it causes fans to become "more passive in their participation in cultural life." Initially, the plethora of music online has the potential to turn fans into relatively passive decision makers. What Schwartz argues is that when choice gets overwhelming for fans, they turn from "choosers" into "pickers." The distinction between these terms "is meant to capture differences in how active and engaged people are as they make their decisions." Choosers are fans who make active choices that revolve around their musical experiences. They critically evaluate the music they listen to and are willing to take the initiative and attempt to uncover songs they will truly like. Their degree of engagement bears fruit, but it is demanding. On occasion, they may even come to the conclusion that none of the songs they have discovered will satisfy them, and they will continue searching. Pickers, on the contrary, are much more passive fans. They do not want to take the time or make the effort to seek out their music, nor will they ever decide that none of the music they are presented with will do. "Picking" is what happens when a fan logs onto Amazon and scrolls through the section of "Customers Who Bought This Item Also Bought." Here, fans are not interrogating their options. They are merely selecting their favorite albums from the musical conveyer belt Amazon provides. Recall again Anderson's argument that too much choice is only "oppressive" when it's ordered wrong, as in a record store, but ordered right, as in Amazon's recommendations, and "it's liberating." The reason fans find this to be so "liberating" is because they are no longer active in the decision-making process, only more passive.

Think about Genius playlists on iTunes, where, according to Apple, "perfect mixes come automatically." The paradoxical effect of a feature like this is that it takes "pickers" — those who rely upon radio to expose them to music — and makes them more engaged and less passive. On the other hand, it also has the same potential to take "choosers" — those who rely on themselves and seek out music — and make them less engaged and less active. "My fear is that overwhelming options turn all of us into pickers, at least much of the time," Schwartz cautions. "If so, it is having an effect that is the opposite of engagement with the life of our society. The paradox is that the more diverse and vibrant cultural offerings become, the more passive and stereotyped the selectors of those offerings become."

"The possibility that overwhelming choice turns people into relatively passive decision makers," Schwartz continues in his research paper, "is the additional possibility that this passivity will carry over into the way they interact with whatever they have chosen." In music fandom, what this relates to is the distinction between casual and true fans, and the orientation they take to the music they listen to. Casual fans are, by definition, passive consumers of music. They have little interest in having a relationship with the artist and feel no need to champion their songs to friends. At the extreme end, it could be said that their experience of music begins and ends with consumption. True fans are actively engaged with the music they experience. "They think about it, they feel it, they talk about it, they bond with one another over it, they interpret it, and they are changed by it," says Schwartz. "To the extent that culture has positive effects on a society, it is surely only when people bring a 'highbrow' orientation to it." To be sure, as Jeremy Schlosberg of *Fingertips Music* argues, "popular music depends upon the existence of casual fans." Their value is underestimated. After all, the existence of casual fans is what makes true fans possible. They are what make the songs of the day a part of our collective identity. Even if casual fans don't speak in the language of the tribe and become actively engaged with it, they still facilitate the capacity for a tribe to continue to grow and gain new members.

The paradoxical effects of choice overload in culture provide insight into why it is that most fans in the digital age are still characterized by their passive consumption of music, especially at a time when many artists are trying to provide them with endless opportunities to become actively engaged in their careers. If the future of the music industry depends on increased prevalence of actively engaged fans — as many thought leaders have argued — then it's worth asking: Is there such a thing as a "paradise of music?"

Paradox or Paradise

In a research paper published in 2003, Professor Alexander Chernev found that "large choice sets are preferred to small ones when people know what they like and thus know what they are looking for." This effect he called "preference articulation." When a fan enters a record store, if they already know what music they like, or what album they are going to buy, they just keep searching until they find it and the more selection the store has, the more likely it is that one of those albums will match their taste. Schwartz writes about Chernev's findings, "a larger choice set increases the chances that what you are looking for actually exists. And finally, technology has enabled us to search through large sets about as rapidly as we search through small ones." In this case then, it could be argued that for the fans who know specifically what music they like, the web has created a "paradise of music." Yet, much of the reason why these paradoxes of choice overload in culture exist is because "the ultimate nature of human taste is irrational and depends on factors impossible to capture with computer systems," says Anthony Volodkin, founder of the Hype Machine. The bias of the Internet-era music consumption system is aimed towards personalization, specialization, and relevance, while also enabling a much more rapid evolution of taste. This has the effect of only blurring the preferences of fans further, making them even less sure about the differences between music they like and that which they do not. Thus, in culture, the effects of overwhelming choice have the potential to cause all fans to opt for the same old thing, rely on filters, and become more passive participants in their musical life. This is not good news. And if the arguments that Schwartz makes about the effects of abundance in the material domain are true of culture as well, he contends that "people will also get less satisfaction out of the cultural choices they make, and they will increasingly opt out altogether."

Not long ago, I made the inference that perhaps this occurrence of fans opting out of the decision-making process is related to file-sharing. "Decision paralysis," in the words of *Made to Stick* co-author Dan Heath, "is a finding from psychology that says: The more options that we're exposed to, the more likely we are to kind of freeze up and go with the path of least resistance." When a fan is faced with a multitude of desirable options, immobilization is possible, and rather than trying to differentiate between the options and deciding which is the best bet (i.e. making a purchase) they either opt out or file-share the music they desire instead. To them, file-sharing becomes the "path of least resistance" — a coping mechanism for decision paralysis — where they can experience all of the options at once and forgo the symptoms we associate with choice overload. The problem with this (beyond the legality of file-sharing) is that once they do have all the options at their disposal, choice overload doesn't just go away. The fan still has to make a decision. After experiencing all of the options, and probably having considered additional ones, they may still opt out entirely and choose not to choose at all.

As we're starting to see, the plethora of music online seems as though it is much more of a paradox than a paradise. Not only does it seem to have the potential to increase the frustration and confusion faced by individual fans, but it also causes them to become more passive rather than more active. And if the future of the music industry really is moving towards the creation of a "middle class" of musicians who market their music and other creative works directly to their fans, they are going to need all of the actively engaged fans they can get. We may never be sure as to whether or not the web has created a paradise or a paradox of music for fans. Nor can we be certain that the benefits of seemingly endless music contributions to society are worth the price of the difficulties fans may experience in making cultural choices.

This brings me to my final, yet most important, question: Shouldn't we also be trying to understand the effects that choice overload has on the satisfaction we get out of the music we already have? Put differently, does having thousands of songs on our iPod lessen the enjoyment we get out of the song that is currently playing? On the iPod, is more music really less?

June 23, 2010

SAVOR YOUR MUSIC: THE EFFECT OF ABUNDANCE IN CULTURE

Thus far, the findings point to the idea that more music is less. As the number of cultural options goes up, the amount of satisfaction a fan derives from any given choice will be lessened. It may even cause them to opt out of the decision-making process altogether. We also found that, in culture, the effect of overwhelming choice has the potential to cause fans to opt for the same old songs as a way to avoid facing unlimited options online and off, to rely on filters like Pandora rather than on themselves, and to become more passive participants in their cultural lives.

Such insights are quite disheartening and run contrary to the long-held beliefs of many, including the viewpoints that Chris Anderson expressed in his book *The Long Tail*. The focus of this essay turns our attention away from our discussion of choice overload and the effects it has on fans when they are purchasing music and brings us to the topic of how overwhelming choice may distress fans when they are enjoying the music they already own. Within the context of the iPod, we will try to discover whether or not storing thousands of songs in our pockets has forced us — as fans — to increase the amount of effort we put into making a decision about what we want to hear and if the consequence of having unlimited options causes us to enjoy any given song less.

"For many of us, the iPod rekindled our dormant passion for music," Steven Levy writes in *The Perfect Thing*. "It made us want to hear more songs, it encouraged us to go out and find new bands to love, it offered new ways to organize music and take it with us." As well, the iPod released fans from the constraints of Top 40 radio playlists and, for the first time, gave them complete control over their musical experiences. Prior iterations, such as the Walkman, only allowed fans to play one album at a time, whereas the iPod granted fans the ability to play any song, from any album, at any time. With the social epidemic of filesharing that occurred alongside the advent of the iPod, the barriers of music consumption fell and the act of collecting music evolved. People gained access to music online and could easily download the thousands of songs required to fill the storage capacity of any iPod. Soon, even fans who previously expressed little interest in the act of collecting music downloaded massive collections of their own.

Now, rather than burning single copies of CDs to give to friends, fans either loaded up their iPod full of music or copied and pasted their entire collections to their hard drive. These common practices and newfound social behaviors had the effect of greatly multiplying the number of music choices many fans faced and left them with the responsibility of navigating collections that expanded far beyond their capabilities of doing so — with any measure of certainty.

When taking into consideration the listening habits of any iPod user I've ever met, it becomes apparent that the girth of their music collections taunts them — most of the time. Either the multitude of songs they encounter when they turn on their iPod is so great that they constantly browse through songs — some they've never even heard — or there's so many highly desirable songs that picking even one of them becomes a task in and of itself, and all of the choices only serve to discourage them further. In this respect, their collections have shifted from being an unalloyed blessing to a burden. What was once the sheer joy of carrying their entire music library in their hand has altered into the responsibility of being a full-time, personal DJ, making selections that best fit their wide variety of moods. Feebly, they try to stumble on the particular song that will make them the happiest.

The reason for this, according to Harvard Psychologist Dan Gilbert in his book *Stumbling on Happiness*, is that people generally err in imagining what will make them happy and, often times, repeat those same errors. Therefore, happiness is rarely as good as people imagine it to be, and rarely lasts as long as they think it will. Someone trying to select the next song on their iPod will usually blunder in deciding what song best fits their emotional state and make the same mistake, with the same songs, many times. When they do finally pick a song, their contentment with it diminishes quickly, causing them to search out the next best song before the one that's currently playing is halfway through. Part of the logic behind this can also be found with the distinction between satisficers and maximizers and the type of decision makers they are.

Maximizing and Music

In choice theory, there are satisficers and maximizers. "We all know people who do their choosing quickly and decisively and people for whom almost every decision is a major project," psychologist Barry Schwartz writes in his book *The Paradox of Choice*. Satisficers are those who "can settle for something that's good enough and not worry about the possibility that there might be something better." In contrast, maximizers are those who "need to be sure that every purchase or decision was the best that could be made."

To give an example, my father is a satisficer, meaning that when we're driving in the car and he's selecting a radio station, he's willing to stop looking once he's found something that's good enough. Oftentimes, it's NPR or some other talk radio outlet. On the other hand, I am a maximizer. This means that when I am in the car with him and it's my turn to pick the station, I often check the other stations to see if something better is playing, even if I'm relatively satisfied with what I'm listening to. The thing is, I want to hear the best song and I strive to achieve that goal. The only way I can ensure that I'm doing so is to explore all of the additional options and to make sure that I'm making the most out of my current musical experience. My tendency to maximize causes me to be nagged at by the stations I didn't have the time to examine. Consequently, I get less pleasure out of the song that's currently on, since, to me, I could've done better.

"The world offers a wide range of options, and something (presently unknown) creates maximizers, and then the two combine to make people unhappy with their decisions," Schwartz writes. "But it is certainly possible that choice and maximizing are not independent of each other." Put differently, it is possible that the excess of music that lives on the iPods of most fans can turn them into maximizers. If this is true, then the proliferation of songs not only makes fans who are maximizers miserable, but it may also make fans who are satisficers into maximizers.

Consider this: Prior to the social phenomenon of the iPod and iTunes, fans had a rather limited degree of control over their listening environments. The amount of pleasure they derived from a musical experience correlated strongly with the quality of the DJ and their ability to select songs that were appealing to the largest audience. So, in navigating their personal collections, fans were beholden to the album format. When making selections of what songs to listen to, the amount of choice they faced was clustered into groups.

The advent of the iPod marked the first truly individualized music experience that was unconstrained by physical formats. It gave them complete control over their listening environment. With that, the iPod and iTunes also helped foster the fracturing of music collections. Fans assembled libraries of music that consisted of individual songs — typically singles. The smaller the collection, the higher the likelihood that the contents reflect the most desirable songs. Though this has the effect of greatly reducing the amount of choices a fan confronts, it still increases the amount of effort that goes into making a decision. The bigger the collection, the more potential there is for fans to feel the effect of overwhelming choice.

All of these shifts in music consumption, mainly increases in autonomy and choice of listening environments, have contributed to turning fans into maximizers, those who seek to get the very best out their musical experiences. But does this make them miserable? To some extent. And it appears to reduce the enjoyment they get out of their music. These shifts seem to have turned those who are satisficers into maximizers. Picking a song that's good enough is harder, it worries fans that they could've done better because they can't set down their iPod and stop scrolling through it.

Why is this? The simplest explanation for this behavioral change and why the iPod may be turning satisficers into maximizers has to do with the very possibilities afforded by the device. "It would seem that the sheer number of musical choices afforded by the iPod can 'liberate' a listener from traditional modes of listening, freeing him or her from the rigid, predetermined song sequences of album," Eric Casero writes in an essay on *Pop Matters*. "This freedom, however, may have the unintended consequence of distracting the listener from his or her current listening experience, thereby diluting this experience by diverting the listener's cognitive focus from the music itself to the musical choices available." One of the more profound things the iPod has altered is our orientation

towards music, causing us to focus on the future of our music experience, more so than on the present. Casero further asserts that, "While
our brains may concentrate some energy on listening to a piece of music,
they are likely, at the same time, to be focusing on possible options for
future listening — options that have only grown in breadth since the
dawn of the digital age." When a fan selects a song to listen to (say it's
three and a half minutes in length, if they aren't shuffling) they will
have to choose the next song before that time has elapsed. Otherwise,
they are at risk of having their music suddenly come to a halt, disrupting
the fluidity of their listening environment. To forgo this interference,
fans will commonly attempt to select the next song while the other is
currently playing. This has the effect of causing them to enjoy the present song less because they have diverted their focus away from it, and
are instead trying to weigh the merits of the next song to occur in the
sequence. Fans aren't "savoring" their music, so to speak. In an effort
to maximize their music experience, it could be said that, in a subtle
way, they are also trying, mostly in vain, to increase the amount of satisfaction and happiness they derive from their music. The problem, of
course, is that in trying to do so, they are getting less as a result.

Overloaded With Choice

As you might guess, fans who exhibit the tendency to maximize their
music experiences are also those who are the most susceptible to the
paradoxes of choice overload. When a fan is overwhelmed by the number of songs on their iPod, it is easier for them to regret a choice if the
alternatives are plentiful than if they were scarce, especially if the alternatives are so plentiful that not all of them could be investigated. This
makes it easy for them to imagine that they could've made a different
choice that would've been better. All the imagined alternatives then in-
duce the fan to regret the decision they made, and this regret subtracts

from the satisfaction they get out of the decision they made, even if it was a good song. However, it was not the best song. To consider the attractiveness of the alternative songs they rejected causes them to become less satisfied with the one they chose, leading them to keep scrolling through their iPod. The more songs they consider, the more missed opportunities add up and collectively diminish the amount of satisfaction they get out of the chosen alternative.

It is likely that fans, too, will opt for the same songs as a way to avoid facing unlimited options and become more reliant on filters — like the shuffle — rather than on themselves, and perhaps all this choice may cause them to become more passive in their participation in cultural life. Part of the logic behind this contention is that as our cultural options proliferate, as neurologist Daniel Levitin suggests, it "causes us not to bond or bind to a particular musical piece." In fact, fans may wind up attached to none of them.

Moreover, Casero argues that, "As technology delivers an increasing number of options for music listening, the music itself becomes increasingly dissociated from any kind of physical medium." This, he contends, has the effect of significantly reducing "the impact that any single piece of music can have on our conscious state because that piece no longer carries with it the same cognitive connections that it would have in previous eras." Consequentially, what happens when fans listen to music on the iPod is that they become engaged with a single object. Before the digital music era, when fans listened to albums, they had to engage with multiple objects, each of which represented the work of a particular artiste. Casero believes that this may change the way we perceive music. "We start to see 'music' as a single totality, rather than something created by multiple individual artists." As a result, the individual identities of these artists begin to dissolve — as do our personal relationships with them.

The other reason: "The thing that made it different for me was that you had to choose," Eliot Van Buskirk writes in *Wired*. "You would have enough for one CD or tape, sometimes, to buy that week. You really had to do research and immerse yourself and read reviews of the stuff, and now you can just get it right away." This utter disparity between "choosing" and "picking" was discussed earlier.

Choosing is the mark of an actively engaged fan, one who critically evaluates the music they want to put on their iPod. The practice is demanding, but it bears fruit. Once in a while, they may even come to the conclusion that none of the above music will get uploaded. Now take someone who file-shares their music and fills their iPod with it. In that instance, they are choosing not to choose at all. They are just picking all the music they might like, which is a much more passive approach. They might be interrogating their options so as to not waste time and bandwidth, but the decision-making process makes them much more passive and likely causes them to become less active in their cultural lives.

Two of the remaining consequences of fans being overloaded with options are the curse of high expectations and self-blame. What contributes to the escalation of expectations among iPod users, beyond their past relationship with radio and MTV, is the amount of choice and control they now have over their listening environment. Outside of the waves of least objectionable, "one size fits all" programming of yesteryear, users are granted complete and utter dictation over their musical experiences. Yet, what this leads to is circumstances that seem to conspire to make their listening sessions less satisfying than they could be, in part because users expect them to be that much better. No one has high expectations of radio stations. Listeners expect to be disappointed with the DJ's choice of music at least some of the time. But when it comes to a user trying to select what music they want to hear in a world of full control and an unfettered surplus of songs, they expect to be pleased with their music decisions all the time.

This creates what could be called "the illusion of the perfect song." It is as if iPod users have convinced themselves they are capable of discerning what the ideal song to match their mood is — whenever they grab the device. The search for this song always ensues much longer than expected and users are typically dissatisfied with the results. Some of the time, users accomplish the magic feat of the perfect playlist. But most often, the labor they put in never aligns with their hopes. In taking the idea of personal programming to heart, users have attempted to maximize their music experience to the point where each moment garners the opportunity to hear the best music possible. They can't tell when a good song is good enough, and to not worry if they could've done better.

Most disconcerting of all is that, in a world of unlimited music options, it is hard to avoid blaming oneself for disappointment. "Our heightened individualism means that, not only do we expect perfection in all things, but we expect to produce this perfection ourselves," Schwartz writes. "When we (inevitably) fail, the culture of individualism biases us toward casual explanations that focus on personal rather than universal factors." He continues, "That is, the culture has established a kind of officially acceptable style of casual explanation, and it is . . . one that encourages the individual to blame himself for failure." Meaning that there is no excuse for failure, both in terms of being able to select "the perfect song" on a personal level and also for having bad taste in music at a collective level.

In his book *The Cult of the iPod*, author Leander Kahney documents what's known as "playlistism." As college student Stephen Aubrey told Kahney, it is "discrimination based not on race, sex, or religion, but on someone's terrible taste in music, as revealed by their iTunes music library." In other words, the choice of what music an iPod user listens to has important social consequences. More so than it did for previous generations.

Already, research suggests that you are what you listen to. "It is now common practice to list your favorite bands on sites like MySpace or Facebook," psychologist Jason Rentfrow explains. "This research shows that, in doing so, many of us are also making clear public statements of who we are and how we should be perceived, whether we are conscious of that or not." Nowhere is this clearer than for iPod users, who carry their libraries everywhere. Except with an excess of music, there is no excuse for bad taste.

All of this has the effect of causing us to enjoy the music we own less and to derive smaller amounts of satisfaction from our iPod listening sessions. Fans love their iPods. Even the music we do own, when there is too much choice, becomes much more of a paradox than a paradise. As fans, if we can't enjoy the song that's currently playing on our iPod, what can we enjoy? The answer to that question, if there is one, feels less clear than it should be.

To be sure, it is certainly not my intent to persuade you that there's too much music out there, online, wherever, as not only would that be heresy, but also I happen to think there's not nearly enough music. Either way, the purpose of this exploration into choice theory, as it applies to the obstacles fans face in the digital age, is to provoke thought. Not to scare anyone into thinking through and through that, in a culture abundant with music, fans are being robbed of satisfaction.

Sometimes, more music is less. Other times, that may not be the case. More important than any of these inferences may be the simple, yet powerful notion that we need to savor our music. This means, much like it does at the dinner table, that we need to set down our forks and really taste the food that's in our mouth. Same goes with the iPod. Set it down, forget all the choices, and just listen.

August 2, 2010

THE HIDDEN CHALLENGES OF SUBSCRIPTION MUSIC

A decade ago, Rhapsody debuted its subscription music service.

Giving fans unlimited music access for a monthly fee appeared to be the answer to the social epidemic of file-sharing that occurred, but fans were indifferent to Rhapsody and it failed to break into the mainstream market.

Apple's iPhone gave subscription music services distribution and portability, but they have failed to reach critical mass due to issues of consumer awareness, user retention, and smartphone penetration.

The problems that subscription services face are much larger though.

Logic tells us that casual fans do not want to use apps that ask too much of them. Yet, in lowering the amount of effort that users must exert in order to build collections, companies take away the opportunities for personalization and customization that are essential to users forming a lasting connection to their music.

In this essay, we are going to expand on this theory and explore why free trials are too short, what service features are essential to converting free users into subscribers, and the importance of preserving the cognitive benefits of music ownership.

Why Free Trials Are Too Short

Upon discovering a subscription service, users are asked if they would like to partake in a free trial. This is intended to help them determine if they like the service and are willing to pay for it. At fourteen days, MOG currently offers the longest trial. But is this enough time?

For core music fans who are looking to experiment, this window of time should suffice. However, for casual fans, there is reason to believe that they need more time.

Core fans are more likely to have music collections already built and are looking to try out features, browse through the selection, and experiment with the discovery tools. Casual fans do not have the same knowledge base and collection. They need to form a long-lasting attachment to the music that they acquire while using a service. Otherwise, once their free trial expires, they may not see the value in becoming a full-on subscriber.

However, recent studies in behavioral economics suggest there are processes through which perceived value can be heightened. The more effort that users exert, the fonder they become of their music collections. Therefore, they value them more. Likewise, once users take ownership of the songs that they discovered while using a service, they will see them as worth more and the cost of losing access to them will feel much greater.

At present, the brief free trial periods that are offered by subscription services do not give casual fans enough time to develop an attachment to and take ownership of their music.

Here is why trials must be extended:

Labor Leads to Love

When fans use a subscription service, their labor is what leads to love. The more actively involved they are in favoriting songs, creating playlists, and fine-tuning their radio stations, the greater they will value them.

In a fourteen-day window, it is much harder for users to harvest the fruits of their labor and begin to see their music collection grow.

Fewer in-depth listening sessions will be utilized, which means that fewer opportunities for customization, personalization, and attachment will be realized. Because of this, users will not reap the cognitive benefits of the IKEA effect, which is a psychological bias that leads us to overvalue the things we have worked hard to obtain.

If the right amount of time and investment is asked of users, they will regard a subscription — the cost of maintaining access to their music — as a more worthy expense.

Pride in Ownership

The more work users put into a service, the more ownership they will begin to feel for it. Once they start acquiring songs and building playlists, slowly but surely, they will develop an attachment to them and perceive them as more valuable.

Sometimes, users claim ownership over their cloud-based collections before they have paid for the pleasure. As the emotions of ownership come welling up, the loss of their songs starts to feel more painful than spending the few dollars required to keep them.

Users rationalize the added expense and conclude that the loss of their collection would be too much to bear. In general, users fail to appreciate how their perspectives will shift once they start viewing the music as theirs and consequently start viewing losing it as a loss. They thought they were only trying the service out for fourteen days, but in fact, they are becoming owners of the music and are unaware of the emotions that it can ignite in them. Of course, the problem is that, for most users, a free trial won't have this effect.

As non-owners, they will still be able to put some distance between themselves and the music of interest and, thus, will view it with less loving eyes and part ways with it more easily.

Real Value Delayed

Unless a user spends lots of time with the service in the beginning, it will be difficult for him or her to see the potential of a subscription. The real value and fun is after a user builds a few extensive playlists, as well as when the recommendation engine really gets to know them.

Once they have experienced the flexibility and customization, they will be more attuned to the possibilities. But without an extended trial, users will be less likely to create playlists and enjoy their unlimited and personalized nature. It takes time for the recommendation engine to learn a user's unique taste and make good suggestions.

With trials as limited as they are, casual fans never experience the potential of a service.

Thresholds May Vary

People have many types of collections — small and big. Some own only a few CDs. Others have obtained hundreds. However, even small-time collectors can be instilled with a sense of pride or ownership if they have crossed a threshold and achieved a degree of completion that satisfies them. A person may own every Metallica album, and nothing else, but still take pride in owning them.

When users are testing out a service, if they do not reach a personal milestone — a designated amount of music — they may not see any value in paying to access it. If they have not collected enough songs, created enough playlists, or felt the experience of having a personalized song suggested to them, they will not view the music on the service as their own. In turn, the cognitive benefits of pride in ownership will not be bestowed upon them. Since core fans are more likely to have collections of their own, it is the casual users who will need the extra time to build collections, and fourteen days will not provide enough chances for these types of users to become proud owners of their music.

Due to these arguments, it is apparent that free trials in subscription services are too short. Even Netflix gives new users a month to test out their offering. For casual fans, a similar — if not longer — duration of time is required for their labor to lead to love and for them take pride in music ownership, to see the potential of a subscription service and cross a threshold that will cause them to overvalue the collection that they have built.

Unfortunately, asking the major labels to allow subscription services to offer extended trials of their music streaming is wishful thinking. They are weary of giving users free music and would not grant leniency in their services based on the royalty fees they would accrue.

For services, lengthening trials is cost prohibitive. They already pay huge overheads. It makes more sense for them to spend that money enhancing their user experience and marketing their product. So that's exactly what they do. If they had leniency from labels or the money to burn, they might consider extending their free trials. But as it stands now, offering a fourteen-day free trial to new users is the best that they can do. Doing otherwise would be financial suicide.

Yet despite these dilemmas, companies like Slacker are making it so that it is not reliant on free trials of its service and along the way, they may convert its users into owners, too.

The Mainstream Cloud

The great paradox of cloud-based music services is that in their attempts to attract casual fans, they may take the effort out of music. In turn, users lose out on the cognitive benefits that effort and ownership provide.

As we have learned, labor is what leads to love, and all people have different thresholds that they must cross before they are willing to take ownership of their music. Once users become owners, their sense of value is heightened. Lastly, it takes time for the real value of a music subscription to be revealed.

To date, the skepticism that surrounds this transition has focused on the viability of the business models and the probability of fans embracing access over ownership. Rarely has anyone challenged the implications of the mainstream cloud itself and how it will alter our relationship to music. The converted, i.e. the utopians, will tell you that unlimited access to music is pure ecstasy. For any cultural shift of this magnitude, though, there is always a downside. Something along the way — no matter how subtle or seemingly insignificant — will be lost. At this point, we do not know what that will be, but it is safe to say that ownership and effort will be further diluted, and if this does occur, the devaluation of music will be accelerated.

The major labels claim that the pricing and abundance of choice given to users will devalue music. That is only half of the story. It is when subscription services increasingly pursue evermore easy-to-use and effortless features in order to appeal to casual fans that music will be devalued. Once the entire history of recorded music is one click away and a customized radio station can be created with yet another click, the real devaluation of music will become apparent. Furthermore, behind all of the delight, something significant will be lost.

Benefits without the Burden

By now, you are probably thinking that the notion of users owning music and exerting effort to get it is a lovely but antiquated ideology. This argument is not lost on me. The young and the digital have never owned music in a tangible form, nor have they exerted effort to get it. To them, there is no difference between a download and a stream. Music is music.

Thus, it would seem as if I am romanticizing the joys and processes of analog culture without addressing the fact that we live in a digital world. These are fair criticisms, which is why this moment matters. In our race to achieve the utmost convenience in our lives, we have embraced technologies without questioning how they may change our relationship to music. Slowly, the barriers to collecting music fell, and each of us became a collector.

In the digital age, subscription music services are leading the charge toward taking the burden out of music ownership. The great paradox is that we are creating an effort-free paradise of music, yet the quality of our music and how much enjoyment we derive from it may actually depend upon effort. The question we must ask ourselves now is this:

Can the burden of music ownership be removed without damaging the benefits?

Let's hope so. Music has always imposed a burden on people. Digital music alleviated many because it costs less, takes up less space, and requires less energy and time. Subscription services seek to further lessen the burden of music ownership, and in doing so, they risk removing the cognitive benefits that it provides. If neither effort nor ownership is present in subscription services, they risk further devaluing music and diminishing user enjoyment.

To be clear, I am not arguing that we must return to the pre-digital era — that somehow the devaluation of music can be stalled. Nor am I saying that users can somehow be tricked into becoming collectors and perceiving music at a higher value. There is no magical formula for subscription music. Rather, I'm contending that we need to be mindful of the future that we are creating for ourselves and the music we love. Our actions have consequences. Not everyone wants to own music. Not everyone wants to bother with effort, either. However, only by engaging with these questions can we differentiate between the future we intend to create and the one that the technologies we are using intend to create for us. Never forget: Music quality is not only determined by bit rate, but our own efforts.

March 10, 2011

CHAOS WE CAN STAND: THE NEW DIGITAL MUSIC ECOLOGY

When I discovered in the seventh grade that I had poor vision, I realized that I would need to get glasses. Not just any glasses though, the specific style that I wanted were those worn by the front man of the rock group Linkin Park, Chester Bennington. They were thick-framed black glasses and in my mind, they looked amazing on him. As it would turn out, the glasses looked less than stellar on me and I got a completely different pair.

Back then, I was an adamant fan of Linkin Park. I knew all the lyrics, saw every music video, and owned all of the albums. I wanted to align characteristics of their identity with my own. The thought of looking like Bennington and wearing his glasses seemed like a logical expression of self.

Members of Linkin Park were not aware of my existence. I was camped out on a farm in the backwoods of North Dakota but I felt a compelling bond towards them and their music. I knew everything about Linkin Park, but they were not privy in the slightest way to the particulars of my life. My relationship with the group slanted more towards the illusion of interaction than any actual social interaction. Social scientists characterize this kind of one-sided relationship as parasocial in nature.

Mass media outlets served as intermediaries between us. If I wanted to see their latest music video, I had to send in requests to TRL. If I wanted to read an interview or hear about the next album, I had to buy a magazine. If I wanted to hear a new song, I had to call a DJ and request it.

Had I come of age during the rise of MySpace's dominance, my understanding and connection to music culture might have been different. Early on, artists used the networking site to peel back the layers between themselves and their fans. They engaged in actual social interaction, forming closer relationships with their fans.

This had the effect of evolving the artist-to-fan dynamic. It redefined the shared bond between the two because artists addressed their fans directly and answered to their concerns. The new digital ecology moves away from the illusion of interaction and towards a real one. Fans can choose to be known to their favorite groups, be engaged, and have a more personalized connection. From here on out, it will be the artists, executives, and those born digital that will mold the landscape of music culture with their attitudes toward technology.

The key differentiating factor between this new ecology and the one that existed prior to the web is the capacity to allow those who are active participants in their own cultural lives to find each other, interact, voice opinions, and create change without being limited by their geographies. This change could be anything from using grassroots, crowd-funding applications such as Kickstarter and PledgeMusic, which assist musicians and provide them with alternative means to fund their creative projects, to connecting directly with artists through social media and networks. Both artists and fans are using those same social tools to advocate and promote the music they love and disseminating it to a wider audience. Fans may also utilize a digital service such as Eventful, which allows them to demand that an artist to play in their area no matter how remote.

All of these tools help to connect fans to the processes of arts creation and enable them to exchange value directly with artists rather than having their interactions mediated solely through a few mass media outlets.

In the book *Born Digital*, law professors John Palfrey and Urs Gasser write, "Make no mistake: We are at a crossroads. There are two possible paths before us — one in which we destroy what is great about the Internet and how young people use it, and one in which we make smart choices and head toward a bright future in the digital age."

For major labels, famous for stonewalling new high-tech innovations and locking up content, the salvation lies in offering music services that are more in step with the emerging social norms of the young and the digital, without hindering the development of the digital ecology of culture that could one day rescue the labels from cultural and fiscal bankruptcy.

Music as Commerce

"When a new technology arrives, it has to get integrated into society somehow," tech-evangelist Clay Shirky writes in his book *Cognitive Surplus*. Between the traditional record industry and the new or "next music business," there is a certain degree of dichotomy in their attitudes toward new technology and their willingness to integrate it into their industries.

From the perspective of journalist and author of 2009's *Appetite for Self-Destruction* Steve Knopper, to correctly characterize this difference in temperament we would first need to define exactly what the next music business is. Knopper poses the question: "Is it what Radiohead did, what Topsin is doing, what Amanda Palmer is doing, what Warner

Music Group is doing, online retail sites like iTunes and Amazon, the loose coalition of free music available on MySpace, Google, Spotify, or even file-sharing?"

We do know that the next music business is not album-centric and that it is a much leaner industry, one that is rife with creative opportunities for artists to pursue new revenue streams. Above all, it is about acquiring fans and the creation of a middle class of artists who are going to have lower margins and smaller profits.

Knopper notes that the traditional record industry is "embracing some of this stuff, with a few decent money making ideas like Vevo and playing Amazon and iTunes off each other leading to cheaper online music for consumers." But he argues that, overall, "the record business could really use a high-tech visionary, somebody who understands that the old model is over, and breaking hits Jimmy Iovine-style isn't going to float the business for the next 30 years."

The paradox is that those in the record industry are committed to solving the problem of financing and distributing recorded music but company executives have devoted themselves to keeping the barriers to music as high as possible in order to keep their old-school solution viable. New technologies like file-sharing disrupt the process through which those operations occur, shifting their business model.

Knopper does make a point to say that he does not think that the record industry is hindering new technology as aggressively as it was fifteen or even ten years ago. Originally, as the new digital ecology emerged, the strategy of executives was to litigate rather than innovate, which is to say that the industry sued everybody and attempted to stamp DRM on all the CDs and digital tracks.

As legal expert William Patry asserts in his book *Moral Panics and the Copyright Wars*, litigation is a poor long-term strategy, which in this case only served to stall the inevitable failure of the record industry's business model. At present, the industry is structured around a top-down, highly centralized "push" marketing model where a few gatekeepers anticipate the demand for their product in the marketplace and finance the production of music from a small number of artists. It's based upon what they want to sell to music fans, not on what fans want to buy. The problem that arises here — when fans become unsatisfied not only with the product being distributed, but the means through which it is distributed — is that in times of change the highly specified, centralized, and restrictive nature of the record industry and their push systems prevent them from adapting.

"The problem now," Knopper continues, "is more a lack of innovation or forward-thinking." Author and industry journalist Fred Goodman agrees. In his book *Fortune's Fool*, he writes "The sorry fact was that record executives had no personal financial incentive to be forward-thinking."

Since the financial incentives of executives (specifically bonuses) are based on chart performance and market share, they became focused on the capitalization of short-term gains in the form of pursuing blockbuster albums. This approach came at the expense of the record industry's long-term stability. What suffers as a result of this mindset of seeing music as solely commerce, is music as culture. Music as art.

This point of view distracted executives further from the real-world ideas and activities through which they might have been able to realign themselves with, not only the technological and societal shifts, but the changes in consumer behavior that had occurred over the course of the last decade. "When institutions fail to distinguish between current practices and the enduring principles of their success, and mistakenly fossilize around their practices," business consultant Jim Collins writes in his book *How the Mighty Fall*, "they've set themselves up for decline."

Executives created a speculative, abstract model by adopting the ethos of MTV, commercial radio stations, and big-box retail outlets. Scrambling to support the creation of blockbuster artists, they disabled the mechanisms through which they might address and correct the collapse of the "real" music industry, which had once operated outside the walls of these media outlets and multi-national corporations.

In the advent of the digital revolution and with the epidemic of file-sharing that ensued, a chaotic yet more genuine digital ecology of music culture is now starting to re-form itself on the web, but this ecosystem — that took decades or more to develop offline — isn't just going to reappear overnight online.

The Digital Dilemma

According to tech-evangelist Clay Shirky, there is now a cognitive surplus in our culture, an excess of free time and talents in the developed world. When considered as a whole, he goes on, this amounts to over a trillion hours a year. He argues in his book, *Cognitive Surplus*, that it hadn't been experienced as a surplus up until now mainly, because before the internet there was no way to pool it together in aggregate and there was no large-scale way to introduce people with disparate yet complementary skills or interests.

With the rise of the web, what we got was a network that was natively good at supporting social communication and participation. What matters now is how the record industry positions itself to harness this surplus.

Shirky argues that the single greatest predictor of how much value can be derived from this surfeit of free time is how much we "allow and encourage one another to experiment, because the only group that can try everything is everybody." In other words, the way to explore and cultivate complex ecosystems like the new digital ecology is to have as many groups as possible try as many things as possible, with the general hope that everyone who does fail will do so in an informative manner.

To Shirky, this is the best method of managing a revolution, a tactic he deems embracing "As Much Chaos As We Can Stand." From his perspective, in order to get the most out of this process, the record industry needs to stop clinging to old models and let "any would-be revolutionary try anything they like with the new technology, without regard for the existing cultural or social norms or potential damage to current social institutions."

This concept of "embracing chaos" leads to the question as to whether the record industry could actually make itself worse off by allowing chaos. Jared Moya, Chief Editor at *ZeroPaid*, says that the only way he could think of the industry being worse off "is if this experimentation leads to a new form of music consumption that it refuses to embrace."

To Rob MacArthur, CEO of the crowd-funding site IOUmusic, the industry would improve if they allowed this to happen, as they could profit from the creative restructuring of their business model, glean the future direction of their industry, and react nimbly by incorporating and profiting from crowd-tested ideas. He says that the key way the record industry may come out of this process negatively is mostly due to "the damage it has and continues to do to their relationships with artists." On the other hand, MacArthur affirms the record industry could be healthier if it took some control of the situation.

Yet, if history tells us anything, there will not be chaos anytime soon. Because the record industry owns a majority of the copyrights to the music they have released, they have veto power over new technologies and the people that champion them. This authority has effectively allowed the industry to stifle innovation by not allowing these startups the rights to use their massive catalogs of music. Without music from the major labels, most music services fail to attain a scalable audience. Even if access is granted, the licensing fees are set at a percentage so high that it often makes their business models unsustainable.

Quite paradoxically, Patry indicates how in the last decade it was not uncommon for the record industry to strangle the online music market, only to later point to the strangled state of the market as a reason not to invest in it.

In stark contrast to embracing chaos, the old-school record industry is founded on a rather different mindset, attempting to manage the digital music revolution. It operates under what Shirky refers to as "Traditionalist Approval." The executives in the record industry — those responsible for the current way of doing things — are the same people who determine the fate of new technologies.

As we have seen, this system has been nothing short of a small disaster.

While attempting to preserve the older form of value in music via physical media and the album format, the record industry has prevented the creation of new value. Rather than incorporating digital technologies into their business, they have either litigated them out of existence or claimed that they foresaw no value in them.

Part of the reason for this, as Shirky suggests, is that "people committed to keeping the current system will tend, as a group, to have trouble seeing any value in anything disruptive." However, these efforts to forestall technological progress are not always out of self-interest. In fact, many record executives would want to defend the tactile nature of physical media and what could be called the "the concerted sonic experience" out of deep and real conviction.

In periods of technological stability, biases in favor of the existing consumption system are good. It's beneficial to have employees think of their jobs as valued by society, even if they aren't. "This sort of commitment is good for morale and leads people to defend useful and valuable institutions," Shirky says. "However, that intellectual asset turns into a liability in times of revolution precisely because those deeply committed to old solutions cannot see how society would benefit from an approach incompatible with older models."

Moya adds that the record industry has "a great deal at stake in maintaining the sort of physical distribution model that has always been its mainstay." For a long time, it has been an industry producing a product that it counts in units sold, "and that's precisely why it's in its current predicament."

Since the days of Napster, many executives, like CEO of Sony Music Entertainment Doug Morris, have said that they did not see these societal and technological changes coming. Because they are not technologists, they were unsure of how to handle the proliferation of digital technologies, the social epidemic of file-sharing, and the fracturing of the album format. In his book *Appetite for Self-Destruction*, Knopper argues that many people at those companies — the Robin Bechtels and Erin Yasgars of the world — saw "the opportunities for working with Napster and marketing music online and were shouting to people like Doug Morris that they should pay attention." Knopper says he would like to see the major labels shift from the old-school record industry executives who were in charge during the Napster era to hiring visionaries and "giving them enough rope to try new ideas and even fail with new ideas." Like Shirky, he believes in letting people try as many things as possible.

The digital dilemma that the record industry now faces is two-fold. On one hand, they must make smart choices and offer music services that are more congruent with the emerging social norms of the young and the digital. On the other, artists and music companies alike need to reconnect with fans and align the right means and tools of participation with the motives of fans so that it is the fans that create civic and communal value.

The record industry should care the most about enabling the young and the digital as innovators to reshape the new digital ecology. It makes sense for fans to be the ones who create public and civic value because these types of value arise most naturally from the fervent devotion of fans. To try to impose the value artificially from the top down is to risk putting the scent of the fake on it.

As innovators, what separates the young and the digital from past generations is that when they have big, ambitious ideas they can implement them on their own without asking for anyone's permission. In the short term, like in the case of Napster and BitTorrent, much disruption is caused and jobs may be lost. But as Palfrey and Gasser argue, soon their "creative destruction will begin to look more constructive than it does today."

Technology Impacts Ecology

As we see, our attitudes toward technology have a great impact on the new digital ecology. However, even if the record industry has seen the light and now wants to embrace the chaos, it will be difficult. So much of the structure that held together our music culture has disappeared: our local record shops and radio stations are almost gone and the audience for recorded music has become fractured to the point where executives cannot simply spend money in hopes that the ecology that corporatism destroyed will re-form from the ground up.

The stakes of our actions are very high. The choices that the record industry is making now will affect how future generations create meaning, how they understand and interact with their cultural objects in the digital age.

In the place of the commercial radio stations and big-box retail outlets that the record industry favored, a "new grass-roots industry is taking shape, though how it will eventually look is anybody's guess," music critic Greg Kot states.

This new, more chaotic brand of digital ecology is fueled primarily by an audience that is scattered throughout the web and has gained a deep enthusiasm for music that they did not even know existed. What it means to be a fan has changed

The Internet enables fans to connect with each other instantly across great distances. It significantly diminishes their reliance on traditional music publications and the PR outlets that power them, and it provides fans with the means to develop relationships worldwide and exist as centers of scenes regardless of their physical location. The Internet also provides an infrastructure which makes it extremely easy to have group discussions which can be archived, allowing the conversations to continue for long periods of time. Most significantly, this ecology gives fans all kinds of new ways to engage with music, artists, and each other because it eliminates all the layers of filters that separated fans from performers.

This shift has also changed what it means to be an artist. The traditional record industry has strongly reinforced a belief that artists should just be artists. As creators of cultural content, artists were told they should not have to worry themselves with how they are engaging with their audience. These activities were viewed as disturbances to their creative energy. But as we know, the age of the aloof artist disconnected from his audience, or not even knowing them at all, is long gone. It is not that there cannot be artists who center mainly on the process of creation, but for every artist that is not willing to get more deeply involved with their careers, there are many, many more that are willing to do the extra work.

"There is nothing that prevents artists from just being artists," says David Dufresne, CEO of the website management platform Bandzoogle. "However, if an artist wants to make a career out of being an artist, then that typically means that the artist will need to find both an audience that is engaged with the artist's creative output, and ways to earn revenue from that engagement."

Thus, it is not only the record industry that needs to stop clinging to old models and embrace "As Much Chaos As We Can Stand" in adopting new technologies. Artists too, those of the old and new digital sphere, share in the same degree of dichotomy in their attitudes toward new technology and their willingness to integrate it into their careers.

Music publicist Ariel Hyatt has argued that part of the reason why artists will not use social media is because it takes too much time, will not put money in their pockets, and has no impact on the real world.

The other reason, according to Dufresne, is that too much conditioning has occurred in the last thirty years — so much so, that many artists refuse to break from existing cultural and social norms. However, others like Amanda Palmer, Zoe Keating, I Fight Dragons, and Ellis Paul are getting it right and letting technology reshape the social interactions they have with their fans. They redefine their roles as cultural creators, as opposed to grasping onto outdated notions of what it means to be an artist.

To Chris Vinson, founder and CTO of Bandzoogle, the concept of artists needing to embrace "As Much Chaos As We Can Stand" in adopting digital technologies "definitely rings true when you look at the larger picture." He argues that by embracing chaos, artists are allowed to "re-invent the way they promote and monetize their art."

"Right now, everything is wide open," says Kevin Breuner, the Marketing Manager at CD Baby. "Artists are able to try anything they want to when it comes to the way they connect with their fans and get their music out."

What the Internet does as a medium is to give artists the opportunity to exchange value directly with their fans, rather than through corporations. It became a platform where genuine bottom-up value creation could occur and where a new digital ecology — one that treats fans as part of the music process and invites them to actively participate inside it — has been able to thrive within chaos.

Rebuilding Our Culture

At first, the lesson here seems to be that the new digital ecology has enabled fans to connect with the artists they love. However, that is only half of the story.

The true potential of it lies in empowering fans to unite with each other. As a teenager, I developed a strong interest in writing poetry and lyrics. Living on a farm a few miles outside of a sparsely populated community, I had no one to share that newfound passion with. Seeking ways to express my interest and meet others looking for the same outlets, I eventually got involved in Linkin Park's message board. Though the discussion there mostly related to the happenings around the band, there was a thread for fans to post their own poetry and lyrics.

However, to become a part of the community you could not just post your own works and hope to get replies. You had to comment on the pieces from other fans and develop a cache of social currency. Bonds developed and authors became friends, vowing to track and comment on each other's works as they appeared. Over time, our interest in Linkin Park faded into the background, and our true intention revealed itself. We wanted to establish relationships with each other. The rock group served as a place to start, a common interest point.

Through MSN, an instant messaging client, and the online forum, we directed a fan experience from various parts of the world that shaped our collective identities both online and offline. The web gave us as fans, a portal for the exploration, expression, and development of our special interests. Our unique personalities and need for individuality led us to colonize a place that we lacked in our everyday lives. Each of us heard Linkin Park on the radio or saw them on MTV but didn't have the means to find other fans. Once found, we discovered our love for music was not the only interest we shared.

Communications scholar Nancy Baym says that it is important to consider that the record industry has only been around for a fraction of the time that music and fans have been around, and if it hopes to be a part of this dynamic, it must accept vast changes. Otherwise, artists and fans will find ways to work around the major labels until the industry, as it now exists, becomes irrelevant. She has also suggested "At a time when the music industry is reeling from changes it barely understands the sorts of activities fans are doing online have the potential to create the culture in which we will all be operating in the future."

The next step the record industry needs to take is to give fans the capability to do something with their cumulative free time, what Shirky called "cognitive surplus." This time around, however, if the record industry's attitudes toward technology hinder the evolution of this digital ecology, there is no second chance. This is the only one they have left.

For the rest of us, artists and fans alike, the opportunity to recast and remake the music industry is enormous. "At a time when so much of the structure that holds together music culture has disappeared," Eric Harvey at *Pitchfork* writes, "fans could take the initiative to create a new one." During the transition from one paradigm to the next, jobs will be lost and artists will be dropped from their labels. Record stores will close. This is unfortunate but necessary.

Long before the creation of this system, music and fans existed. Jared Moya, Chief Editor at *ZeroPaid*, concurs: "How the dust settles is anyone's guess, but one thing is certain: artists and music fans will always be around," he says. "Recorded music is a relatively recent construct that oftentimes had sinister relationship with both artists and fans, the former falling prey to unscrupulous contracts and record deals, and the latter to unrealistic pricing and overcharging."

Now that music has exposed itself to be a bad growth industry, we can get back to our core objective. What we do with this opportunity will be determined largely by how well we are able to reward artistic creativity, fan participation, and the rebuilding of our culture. Rather than searching for ways to patch up the past, we must construct an infrastructure for the future and lay the foundation needed to nurture the emerging digital ecology and create a more sustainable and healthy middle class of musicians that the listening public can support.

It may seem like the record industry turned from prosperity to chaos almost overnight. But the crash that occurred with the advent of Napster and the social epidemic of file-sharing, the fracturing of the album format and the demise of mass marketing was years, perhaps even decades in the making.

It is easy to point fingers, to scapegoat the fans and the companies and sites who desired to quench their thirst for free music. But there are more subtle and sophisticated technological and societal shifts occurring, which are much bigger than fans sharing and downloading music without paying for it.

The record industry is collapsing, and ultimately this may be good thing. If it dies, it will make room for a new ecology to rise up in its place. This death may be painful to watch, but if major labels refuse to embrace the chaos, then it is our calling — as would-be revolutionaries — to create the chaos. As cartoonist Hugh MacLeod once said, "This is it. Fight like hell." Create the chaos. We need you.

April 6, 2010

THE RISE OF CAPTURE CULTURE: HOW APPS ARE REVOLUTIONIZING MUSIC COLLECTING

For decades, the question, "What song is playing?" plagued music fans. If a DJ failed to announce an artist's name or the song's title, fans were left to their own devices to figure it out (usually singing, humming and/or reciting misremembered lyrics to bemused friends or annoyed record-store clerks). Often, people accepted the music playing through the speakers in TV shows, movies, and bars as background ambience, because they lacked a means to identify a song and discover the artist behind it.

Today, of course, fans can get that info and lots more immediately: They can pull out their smartphones and use music-ID apps like Shazam and SoundHound to instantly name a song and gain a wealth of information about the music-artist bio, video, song purchase links, lyrics, tour dates, and much more. "And, in turn, [a fan's] senses are heightened," says Keyvan Mohajer, the CEO of SoundHound, "because music they hear around them is in fact 'capturable' and therefore interactive."

What's significant about this "interactivity" is that music-ID apps empower fans to turn any passive listening session into an active one, where they lean forward and learn more about an artist.

But that's not all fans can do. Shazam and SoundHound have partnered with the subscription music service Spotify, enabling users to play identified songs and add them to their library.

Shazam rolled this feature out to premium users in January, months before Spotify launched stateside, and soon offered it to free users too. SoundHound, on the other hand, enabled their "Play Now In Spotify" option in August, but only European users have the option now. While this feature might seem minor, it marks a critical turn in the way fans collect and discover music.

Traditionally, we think of music collecting as the act of acquiring music through a purchase, but that's quickly changing. With Spotify integrating with music-ID apps, it gives fans a new option: capturing. When a Shazam or SoundHound user tags a song playing on the radio, they can now bring it into Spotify and listen to it there. If they so choose, they can also add it to their music library, making it easy for fans to capture and collect songs.

As the long-heralded shift from owning music to accessing it takes place, we're also slowly moving from collecting music to capturing it. Music service MOG, for instance, recently launched an app feature called "Moggles." Users can hold their phone up to any picture of album art and "we identify and add it to your collection or let you start playing it," says MOG CEO David Hyman. "You can go to a record shop or be at a friend's house and see a CD cover or vinyl, and snap a picture." It even works when you "hold it up to little images of album art on your computer screen," he added.

Welcome to capture culture: Where music is not solely bought from a store and collected in our home, but captured from our environment through mobile apps and instantly stored in the cloud. This shift is also emerging online. "Soon, we should see the 'add-music' button adjacent to songs and videos on sites around the web," says technology entrepreneur and consultant Bruce Warila.

The add-music button "will enable music fans to collect songs for subsequent streaming to any connected and capable device." Connecting the button to search results and blog entries would make it easy "for fans to add songs to their music libraries," Warila continued.

Currently, neither Google nor Microsoft's Bing have an "add-music" button in search results, but this may change. Google's new music blog, Magnifier, enables readers to add free music downloads to Music Beta, its locker service that lets fans upload music to the cloud and listen to it on the web or Android device.

The potential for converting the web into a music library, however, has not gone unnoticed. Exfm, which launched back in 2010, provides fans with this service. Once installed, the Google Chrome extension operates in the background and alerts users when music on a site is available to be played.

If you visit *Pitchfork.com*, for example, Exfm finds songs on the website and organizes them into a playlist, in the order they appear on the page, ready to be listened to. If a song is found and the extension is opened, users can play, bookmark, and share it. In time, Exfm may offer a "Play in Spotify" button too, transforming the service from a browser extension to an extension of music collections themselves.

Eventually, this could change the entire process of experiencing music. "It makes the collecting of MP3s seem unwieldy. It makes file-sharing seem so Oldsmobile," says Warila. "It displaces today's music widgets. It opens up a world of possibilities for discovery and recommendation. And, it makes the notion of a distribution middleman a thing of the past."

The concept behind Exfm, of course, goes far beyond the web. Several geosocial music services let fans to assign music to places and discover songs in their smartphone app.

Raditaz enables users to link music stations to locations. A local concert venue or coffee shop could, perhaps, create programming that highlights area acts and designate it to their building, giving fans a way to sample music from upcoming shows.

Similarly, Herd.fm gives users the ability to tag locations with songs. When they open the app, it locates their position and places them on a map, showing the music available in the area.

Once these services or others like them take off, an app that identifies geosocial media links and pulls them into a player, like Exfm, may emerge, alerting fans when music is ready to be discovered in their area. And with a button click, these songs will be captured, opening up the potential for the world itself to be turned into a music library.

All of this has vast implications. "Collections will become a short-term phenomenon on the web, captured to share with friends across multiple services and will be indicative of a moment in time, as opposed to a library built up based on a lifetime of listening and curating music for yourself," says Charles Smith, the founder and COO at Exfm. "Unlimited access to almost all the music available puts the focus on discovering what to listen to now, as opposed to what to keep." And ultimately, fans will discover what to listen to next by checking out what their friends are capturing in real time, through in-app activity feeds, as well as by tuning in to what people around them are listening to.

"Music collectors will not become extinct; they will become increasingly rare, like professional photographers whose collections have special value," SoundHound CEO Mohajer adds. "Meanwhile, everyone will become 'music and sound capturers,' and the bulk of those songs captured will be enjoyed for immediacy or bookmarked for later enjoyment."

As fans move from owning music to accessing it, from collecting songs to capturing them, it represents a major development in the digital music revolution, as significant as the MP3 and file-sharing. In a way, the rise of capture culture also signals a wistful return to the cassette era, wherein fans captured their favorite songs off radio and shared them with all their friends, bringing everything full circle.

Every radio station listened to, TV show watched, website visited, and event attended now presents fans with an opportunity to grab songs and sync them to their library, as well as, Smith continues, "be a part of a crowd that's sharing music without any other relationship other than great music."

The scope of capture culture, though, is much wider than music. Any passion that a community of people shares — from reading books to watching movies to going shopping — is a moment that's open to being captured and shared through Facebook and Twitter with friends, family, and fellow enthusiasts.

Media and products are the leading currencies in capture culture, but the real product is storytelling.

SoundTracking, another app, combines elements of both music-ID and geosocial. When a user captures a song, they're encouraged to add context to their experience and tell a story about where they were when heard it and what they were doing. In other words, capture culture isn't solely about sharing musical moments, it's about sharing life moments, and music is just one part of a larger story.

September 12, 2011
Copyrighted 2013
Prometheus Global Media
105258:1013AT

WHY MOST MUSIC APPS FAIL

"If I love a music app, it's the kiss of death," says one music fanatic turned top-level digital music executive, who asked to remain anonymous. "No normal person will use it."

In other words, if a music fanatic finds a "music problem" interesting enough to solve, it doesn't mean that the solution will be a workable business, or that anyone beyond a few other music fanatics has this problem to begin with.

And yet, new music apps get released every week. Many make a huge splash, become the talk of technology blogs and are never heard from again. The truth is that most music apps fail — fail to live up to their initial hype, fail to generate profit, and fail to become "the next Pandora."

While such popularity is not everyone's goal, the task of fixing the music industry is not short of hands, as it still captivates many young, bright minds. Trouble is, many of these would-be saviors are technologists in search of a problem — and oftentimes they solve ones that no "real" person has.

Concert-listings site Songkick recently released an app. Once installed, it scans your music library and syncs the artists you like with those that are touring in your area, creating a calendar of upcoming shows. In the first two weeks, the app surpassed 100,000 downloads. While tracking concerts is a relatively a "music fanatic" activity, it's a behavior that could translate over to the mainstream market.

Music-ID app Shazam also falls in this practical-use category; it enables fans to identify what song is playing on the radio or TV. While it likely started as a "techie solution" to a music-fanatic problem, it caught on — in part — because it solves a real-world dilemma. Since, a "Shazam Friends" feature has been added; it connects the app to Facebook and lets users share what music is discovered.

A similar app is Soundtracking; it identifies songs too, but it goes a step further, allowing them attach a location, photo, or written description. As Soundtracking CEO Steve Jang puts it, the app lets fans share their "musical moments." This difference, while small, matters. New users are attracted to Shazam based on their interest in identifying songs, and a byproduct of that — if they so choose — is self-expression.

So while these apps relate in functionality, their user incentives couldn't be more different. Given that Shazam boasts nearly 150 million users, it's clear the app has crossed over and entered the mainstream market. But Soundtracking is still a new app — will it be as successful? And if not, why? What makes Soundtracking a great lens to explore the success and failure of apps through is that it sits at the border of a fanatic interest and human desire.

Those most compelled to express themselves through music — by nature — are fanatics. Thus, it makes sense to develop an app that targets them. But still, the practical use of Soundtracking may elude the mainstream market. It's unclear if casual fans seek an app to share their "musical moments" with. And herein lies the trouble with most music apps nowadays: It's doubtful that casual fans would want to use them because they're overly specialized and offer a solution to a problem they don't actually have.

In developing new music apps, technologists often underestimate the vastness of the chasm between themselves and real people because they're unable to see past their fanaticism. This "music bias" causes them to "make the flawed assumption that the way [they] consume, discover, enjoy and communicate about music is the same way everybody else does," says Stephen Purdham, CEO and founder of the music service we7. Techies and fanatics "project what they love and want into a belief that it is what everyone else will want and that everyone is at the same level of understanding and passion."

Initially, the enthusiasm of technology writers suggests that this app is the next big thing... and then, nothing. Instead, the "chasm" swallows the app — as author Geoffrey Moore famously explained — and the mainstream market never emerges.

In his book *Crossing the Chasm*, Moore advises high-technology companies to target a very specific niche market, force out any competitors, and then "use it as a base for broader operations." This tactic may work well for Apple, but an app is not an iPod. Developers often take the niche market approach with music apps — and here's the key part — not realizing that they're in a niche market to begin with. An app often starts as a shared interest between techies and fanatics — i.e. the early adopters. And then, in isolation — away from real people — it gets developed. To "cross the chasm" between the early adopter and the mainstream market, as Moore wrote, companies often must make new technology more practical in use. Otherwise, the app, in this case, may not catch on if casual fans see no benefit in using it.

"Everyone is chasing the music fanatic with discovery and social music, rather than the listener who loves music but wants their music being played easily without barriers and without effort," Purdham adds. The problem is that techies and fanatics often interact with each other within specialized domains. This, in turn, creates a mindless feedback loop.

"With respect to music in particular it is important to remember that the majority of fans are passionate only about the music," says Kevin Leflar, CEO and President of officialCOMMUNITY. "Listening to their favorite music may be an entirely personal experience for some. They don't care what other people think about the music they listen to any more than they wish to share their own experience with it." This cold water gets poured on new developers sooner than later: the majority of people love music, but that's it.

Pandora, in contrast, succeeds because it ignores the needs of music fanatics. It doesn't do too much. Users have little control over stations and the music can be repetitious — with too few skips. But to a casual fan, that's fine. They're not upset if Pandora repeats a song. They don't notice when the playlist meanders. And most of all, they don't want more settings: Pandora just works, and that's what they like about it.

Initially, Pandora attracted fanatics, but it sought to serve casual fans. It solves a problem they have. In a busy world — with less free time to discover music — they look to Pandora to expose them to new artists. All other functions are hidden or excluded from the app. This simplicity may frustrate fanatics — who always want more — causing them to move on. But it pleases most people. As Pandora deepens its stake in the car market, it will grow an ever more mainstream base.

Another custom radio app that's posed to become popular is Jelli. It lets users take control of web and broadcast radio stations in real-time, sharing the experience together. In short, the app lets users vote for their favorite songs to be played using "Rockets" and to blast lesser songs out of the playlist using "Bombs." Given that the desire to get ones songs played on radio is as old as radio itself, it's clear that Jelli taps into an emotion shared by fanatic and casual fans. In June, two broadcast radio stations in Las Vegas handed all of their programming over to Jelli — for the first time. Starting out, fanatics will likely be a driving force in app use, with casual fans lurking right behind. As word of mouth spreads and the app catches on though, Jelli may even conquer the chasm, but doing so is not everyone's end goal.

"Much of innovation happens through failure," says *Hypebot.com* founder Bruce Houghton. "Many music apps never reach the iPods of casual fans, but the ideas behind them are often built into others that do, which pushes the music-tech space forward." He believes that, "learning to create and embrace chaos [in the music industry] is better than fighting it."

This mindset of "embracing the chaos" is shared by Dave Haynes, the VP of Business Development for SoundCloud and founder of the music technology event Music Hack Day. At the event, a motley crew of developers, music geeks, designers, and hackers gather to build apps, mobile, software, hardware, and art in a twenty-four hour period-anything goes as long as it's related to music-tech.

"New possibilities and ideas can be explored quickly and affordably," says Haynes. "Huge infrastructure and setup costs are no longer a consideration, with little upfront investment or capital outlays required." So while a majority of the "hacks" that emerge out of the event may only appeal to a niche market, having the ideas interjected into the music industry is often better than not. Later on, the synthesis of several music fanatic "hacks" may turn into an app that becomes "the next Pandora" in terms of mass-market use.

But, as Houghton succinctly summed up: "Few niche music products create profitable markets."

August 17, 2011
Copyrighted 2013
Prometheus Global Media
105258:1013AT

HOW SIRI COULD TRANSFORM MUSIC

The launch of the Apple iPhone 4S has people raving about Siri, the talking-assistant app. It lets users speak into their devices and the app fulfills requests like scheduling plans or replying to text messages. But it also works with music.

In the Apple video trailer for Siri, a person in running clothes asks the app to queue up his running playlist, and seconds later, the music starts. At first, this feels like a gimmick, but if and when Siri becomes integrated with music apps — such as Shazam, TuneWiki, Songkick, Pandora, and Spotify — it could transform music and the way people interact with it.

Currently, if a user wants to identify a song (the "problem"), first they must know that music-ID apps like Shazam and SoundHound exist (the "solution"). Then they must install one of the apps and understand how it works before they can tag a song that's playing on radio or TV.

But what if Shazam were linked to Siri? A user could ask Siri "What song is playing?" and it could prompt to install Shazam or another service, and once completed, Siri would work directly with it, cueing it to automatically identify a song the next time it is asked.

In this scenario, the user only needs to know they have a problem and it's up to Siri to solve it — and as time passes, the process by which it can offer solutions will only get smoother. At this point, there are several hoops to jump through in order for the user to get the result they want. But if music-ID ever became a standard iPhone feature, Siri could instantly return the desired answer.

Most music apps fail because they solve problems that not enough people have, or are sufficiently aware of. With Siri, Apple will continue to provide solutions to problems people don't know they have in the first place.

And this is why Siri could revolutionize music. Most people don't care about individual apps — they care about the problems they solve and, often, the time that can be saved. Indeed, it removes even thinking about apps from the equation — and makes them work more like iPhone features than pieces of software.

If an iPhone user asks Siri what the lyrics to "Don't Stop Believin'" by Journey are, many people won't care much whether TuneWiki or any other app fulfills the request. All that matters to them is that their request gets fulfilled in a timely manner, and that they're soon happily singing, "Just a small town girl, living in a lonely world." Similarly, if a user is seeking concert listings for the night, which match up to the songs on their iPhone, they're unconcerned whether Songkick, Bandsintown, or Ticketmaster produces the results as long as they get them fast and accurately.

Siri fundamentally changes how iPhone users think of apps, which is the point. "It's our job as technologists to make the most efficient and effective product for the end-user," says RootMusic founder and CEO J Sider, who says he admires Apple. "We should be the ones in the background doing the magic, not taking any credit for how incredibly intricate the technology in the background works."

This is not to say that brands don't matter — because they do. People will gravitate toward trusted brands that deliver consistent results in a high-quality manner. Rather, the crux of the argument here is that people don't have "app" problems; they just have problems. Dozens of music companies have been created in recent years that solve problems that, for the most part, most people aren't aware of or aren't much concerned about. But if apps are linked to Siri — eliminating many of the steps between problem and solution — the gap between the problems and solutions will narrow dramatically.

So how many music-related problems does a casual fan actually have? If you think about it, there are actually several: They want to identify and buy songs, look up lyrics, find out what concerts are happening nearby and when, listen to and discover music passively (think: Pandora), request videos and songs on-demand actively (think: Vevo and Spotify), and share songs with friends. Offering an iPhone user instant solutions to these common problems — without them having to necessary understand how they're being solved-shifts the paradigm of music listening and discovery entirely.

Shazam and Pandora aren't just apps; they're features. To use them, a person should only need to know that they want to identify a song or listen to a custom radio station and-like magic-the desired process should occur. Siri can be the genie who makes it happen.

This is the Steve Jobs dream: Technology should work like magic — and consumers should be dazzled by the show, unconcerned how the trick-at-hand is being performed. Speaking of the iPhone and its multi-touch screen display, Jobs emphasized that the feature worked, never alluding to the complex technology that makes the feature work. He simply said, "It works like magic."

October 19, 2011
Copyrighted 2013
Prometheus Global Media
105258:1013AT

FOUR WAYS TO MAKE FACEBOOK
MUSIC A LOT BETTER

Over-sharing on Facebook is certainly nothing new, but the site's new music-sharing option has taken the practice to a new extreme, alarming more than a few people we know in the process.

Once a user adds Spotify or iHeartRadio to their timeline, listening to music equals sharing the activity with friends, automatically and in real time. It's no longer an action, but an afterthought — a decision made when you sign up that now happens every time you hit the play button — and has probably inadvertently outed more than one closet Justin Bieber fan.

This practice, of course, is no mistake — it will certainly help Facebook to gain more insight into its 800-million-plus active users and sell that data to advertisers. But this version of music-sharing is one of many. For Facebook Music (not its official name, but we'll call it that for the sake of convenience) to become all it can be, it should improve the quality of its music-activity feed by taking cues from companies like Pandora and SoundTracking.

Days before the rollout of Facebook Music at f8, Pandora — which was noticeably absent from the list of partners — launched a new website with an increased emphasis on music sharing. In it, a new music-activity feed is subtly displayed. What it highlights, however, differs greatly from Facebook Music.

Pandora lets users opt which friends they want to follow, and it only shows the stations they've tuned into and the songs they gave a "Thumbs Up" to during a listening session. On Facebook, however, listening activity appears in Ticker as it occurs. Then in the music app section, a breakdown of the artists, albums, and playlists that friends have listened to is displayed.

Both feeds are similar in concept, but diverge in their contents. Arguably, though, Pandora has created a better product for casual listeners than Facebook, because it provides the highest yield of potentially great songs to discover while demanding the least investment of a user's time.

Listening doesn't equal liking. By only showing the songs a user gives a "Thumbs Up" to, Pandora reveals the songs friends liked enough to say so — and want to hear again — whereas Facebook forces us to wade through all of the music they listened to, whether or not they liked it.

That's the difference between Pandora and Facebook: one strives to save a user time — by making it easy for them to discover music — while the other seeks to take up more. Presumably, this is not a mistake, but a tactic. The goal for the first stage of Facebook Music appears to be to get as many users as possible to supply their music data. Once the feed is populated with listening activity and has been monetized by deeper ad-targeting, Facebook will likely make strides to improve their feed's quality, with the intent of getting users to spend even more time on the site.

But to do this, Facebook should highlight a broader array of listening activities. Currently, the feed shows, say, 16 Kiss songs that a friend played, which makes sense, because he's an avid Kiss fan. But which of the songs has he listened to the most and did he add any of them to his library? Facebook doesn't say and it may never tell, but context helps users sift through the noise and discover songs.

Direct-sharing from services to Facebook doesn't show up in the feed either. While this type of user sharing is more out of self-expression — more to make a statement about themselves, similar to a Facebook status update, than to recommend a song music to friends — it should be brought into the feed, because it adds an element of a storytelling.

In this regard, Facebook Music has some catching up to do — and SoundTracking, a mobile app, provides insight into how it might get ahead. In effect, what the app lets users do is share their musical moments with friends — what music they like to dance to, work out to, listen to while stuck in traffic, etc. SoundTracking enables users to tell these stories by linking a location, photo, and message to a song and then the app sends it out as a status update to Facebook, Twitter or Foursquare.

Facebook lets users do a similar thing when they check into a location — i.e. tag the place, who you're with, and add a photo — so it's possible they may let users tie songs to their status updates too. This sharing and storytelling is important and would add more color to Facebook's feed, but it has a drawback.

In the race to make music more social, Facebook and the services it counts as partners will learn this: A person's desire to share music will always be greater than their friend's willingness to receive it. When two friends share music, it's typically done in a thoughtful and intimate way. You find a song that you think they'll like and share it. Even if they don't like it, they still derive pleasure from knowing you thought of them.

But Facebook Music runs contrary to this dynamic. One friend decides to add a music service to timeline and share their music activity with their friends — without considering whether they wish to be shared with. Once the updates appear, it's then up to the friends to embrace them or mark them as spam — not the greatest user experience.

By taking the burden of sharing music off the plates of some users — in enabling what Facebook founder and CEO Mark Zuckerberg refers to as "frictionless" sharing — it shifts the hassle of dealing with the updates to others and creates an entirely new tension.

A better feed may resolve this issue, and Facebook is likely working on this and many other ideas now. But if you've surrendered your listening data to Facebook — by adding a music service to timeline — then its venture into music is already a success. The company has your listening data and can sell it to advertisers. How much a user and their friends enjoy the listening activity displayed comes second.

"That's because on Facebook, we're not the customers," writes media theorist and author Douglas Rushkoff on *CNN*. "We are the product."

November 2, 2011
Copyrighted 2013
Prometheus Global Media
105258:1013AT

SPOTIFY MUST WIN HEARTS TO GROW SUBSCRIBERS

Spotify, the online music service, has added a free, ad-supported radio feature to its iOS apps, which allows listeners to create and play music stations — akin to what Pandora offers — for as long as they want.

The need for Spotify to develop a radio service, some suggest, stems from its strategy of "attracting users with free, ad-supported services who can be converted later into paying subscribers." While this may be true, Spotify also realizes that a radio service will allow it to appeal to casual listeners as well as the service's more avid core users.

The success of Pandora, after all, lies in the simplicity of the service and passivity that it allows. You can click play and let the service do the rest, without the need to engage further if you don't want to.

By contrast, Spotify's primary on-demand service requires more work: installing apps, searching for songs, creating playlists and the like. It's designed for active listeners who want control and access, not those who prefer to click a button and listen to whatever comes on.

But the truth is that many listeners do interact with Pandora, tailoring their experience by giving songs a thumbs-up or thumbs-down.

According to the company, users did this over 10 billion times by last year, and such numbers have led many of us — including Spotify — to wonder whether people would be willing to pay Pandora to access to their liked songs. The idea is provocative, but it's still unclear whether such access appeals to casual listeners.

Herein lies the problem: Spotify wants to attract more users with a radio service, but since these additional users are likely more passive, the company must approach and serve them differently from their core audience if they want to earn their business. But what exactly does it take to convert casual listeners into paying subscribers? Is it Spotify as a service, or is it something more?

When pundits talk about owning music being a better experience than accessing it, they often fail to take into account that most people never owned music to begin with, and that a "personal music library" is largely a fanatic concept meaningful to only a minority of listeners. So when a tech-savvy listener counters by extolling the virtues of Spotify and accessing music, it's easy to view this "argument" as larger issue, when it's really a small one.

The digital music revolution and the rise of file sharing certainly encouraged many listeners to hoard as many songs as their discs and iPods could hold, but these are stockpiles, not possessions. Thus, we need to view casual listeners — especially the young and the digital — as people who have never owned much music, and this view should give Spotify some hope of persuading them to use its radio product.

Many, including Spotify rival Slacker Radio, believe that the key to cracking the subscription music sector lies in combining a radio service with an on-demand one, because it allows casual listeners to "like" their favorite songs on music stations and grow a sizable list of them, which one can imagine they would soon want to cue up at will. As interest in doing so grows, such listeners will, presumably, be easily swayed into paying to access their list of favorite songs on demand.

For this happen, however, a listener must take ownership of their music and form a long-lasting bond with it. The amount of time and effort that they invest in Spotify Radio, research suggests, will correlate with how much they value their songs, and before "pride in ownership" can happen, a certain threshold must be passed. Put simply, labor — i.e. listening to and liking lots of songs — is what leads to love, but only if a listener labors enough.

Unfortunately, Slacker, which did combine its radio service with an on-demand one, has proved the potential downfalls of this approach. When you listen to music stations and like songs, they stockpile under the menu option "Favorite Songs," both on the website and in the mobile app. The result, if you've used Slacker Radio for awhile, is an unsightly, seemingly endless artist listing, with only a single song indexed under each, which makes for clumsy and awkward navigation.

"There is a delicate trade-off between effortlessness and investment," says author Dan Ariely in his book, *The Upside of Irrationality*. "Ask people to expend too much effort, and you can drive them away; ask them for too little effort, and you are not providing the opportunities for customization, personalization, and attachment."

Spotify shouldn't just try to recreate Pandora; it must redefine it. Along the way, the service could socialize the fanatic concept of a "personal music library" or entirely reinvent it, but to win hearts, it can't be all thumbs.

June 29, 2012

THE "NEW" PANDORA: BLUE OCEAN TO BLOODY WATER

In late 2010, Pandora set out to create a new Internet radio experience.

Pandora wanted to rebuild the popular service to be "faster, easier, and more social" while remaining familiar to longtime users. By July 2011, Pandora started to roll out its new site to subscribers, collect their initial feedback, fix programming bugs, and make further improvements.

Months later, the "New Pandora," which now allowed users to share songs with friends and learn more about favorite artists, launched for everyone. After over a year of testing and perfecting the user experience, Pandora finally released brand-new mobile apps for iPhone and Android in October 2012.

The journey from "clean sheet of paper" to "entirely new Pandora" took over two years to pull off. For the first time, the Oakland company provided a consistent listening experience and feature set across every platform. Most recently, it also introduced a TV-centric service for gaming consoles.

It's indisputable that Pandora is a product for the mainstream market. It has over 200 million registered users in the United States — 70 million of whom tune in every month. Its dead-simple interface and tightly refined stations have proved a winning combination for music listeners.

If you have a commute that you want to fill with music, Pandora will cue up 30 minutes of songs that sound like Imagine Dragons. The similarity may soon veer toward banality, but the odds are that you will enjoy the music.

By now, the criticisms of Pandora have become well worn: repeated songs, little variety, limited skips, and frequent ads. The upside to the popular service (or why listeners tolerate the latter) is that it does the work, tailors the mix, suggests new bands, and maintains a mood. The convenience of Pandora, in other words, seems to outweigh the trade-off of having a limited experience.

As time goes on, though, that strength has become a weakness.

Take the song "Odds Are" by Barenaked Ladies, for example. If you click around the social charts in Twitter #Music's mobile app, you can find the catchy new rock single pretty easily, and if you're paying subscription fees to Spotify or Rdio, you can listen to it repeatedly. But here's the rub: It's still very difficult for Pandora users to stumble upon "Odds Are" and fall in love.

The "filter bubble," as author and activist Eli Praiser calls it, prevents users of Pandora and other such services from being exposed to songs outside their personal universe of recommendations. If you aren't in the orbit of Barenaked Ladies or similar artists, the "chances are so small" (as the lyrics go) that you'll find that song.

This lament about Pandora's lack of serendipity has been leveled against it many times before, but its "musical cocoon" is becoming harder to ignore.

Erin McKean, founder of the online dictionary Wordnik.com, eloquently stated in her 2007 TED Talk that "Serendipity is when you find things you weren't looking for, because finding what you are looking for is so damn difficult." On Pandora, discovering songs that sound like "Odds Are" is the easy part, but uncovering the hidden gem itself is damn difficult.

More worrisome is that Pandora is also bad at serving up favorite music.

Popular songs by seed artists frequently appear on radio stations, latest singles emerge in relevant places, and "Quick Mix" offers a singular listening experience with greater variety. But that's all. There's no way to solely listen to favorite songs, discover music by unexplored artists, delve into a stream of loved tracks by relevant users, or hear the latest songs by favorite artists.

To be fair, these are ideas that may not appeal to the widest market; they may have failed to gain traction upon research and testing.

If that's the case, that casual listeners don't care about these things, it makes sense. But it's still a missed opportunity, as helping listeners find out when favorite artists release music is a valuable utility that no one does perfectly.

Personal discovery should be integrated into the stations you engage with; it should not be work or create work; it should play out naturally and happily.

But the "real risk" for Pandora, says Max Engel, VP of Product at web publisher SpinMedia, is that "music recommendation is becoming increasingly commoditized." When rival companies like iHeartRadio and Spotify can leverage the music intelligence platform built by The Echo Nest to develop comparable experiences without considerable investment, it makes differentiation for Pandora difficult while making its "Music Genome" database look quaint.

Mr. Engel also worries that Pandora "solves a feature problem, but not a service one." Spotify and Rdio have radio features, he says, so users have "little reason" to leave their primary service to get a radio experience.

There is a belief that Pandora has cultivated deep loyalty among music listeners, and that the switching costs of leaving the popular service for a rival would be too high. But are they? A student will abandon Pandora once she notices that more of her friends are on Spotify Radio. A father will switch from Pandora to Spotify Radio because it plays fewer commercials. A gym-goer will leave Pandora for Spotify Radio because it has far more variety.

The new Pandora suffers from the same old complaints: It has blocked a few fatal blows, but it's near a thousand paper cuts. Tim Westergren has built a single island in a bloody ocean, and it's showing signs of deep erosion.

July 24, 2013

ADVERTISING INDIE: EARBITS HELPS BANDS FIND FANS

It's easy for bands to distribute their music, but hard to market it. They can pay to get their songs in the right places (iTunes, Amazon, and Spotify) but it's unclear how to get them heard by the right people. Earbits, a Los Angeles-based startup, aspires to turn their radio service into an ad platform where bands can buy airtime and gain exposure for their songs and upcoming live performances.

While the web-music sector is crowded with established services like Pandora and Spotify, Earbits stands out because it focuses solely on emerging artists and provides fans with a compelling way to discover them. The service offers genre stations, which are common, and has many features which aren't. For instance, if you log into Earbits using Facebook, the service pulls your friends into a toolbar and sorts them by who'd most enjoy hearing the song currently being played. If you click on one of your friends, a window opens up, which allows you to post the song on their Facebook wall.

Most interesting, though, are the ways in which Earbits nudges their users to engage more deeply with bands. While you listen to a song, you can scroll beneath the fold on the website and find information about the artist, including a bio, discography and tour dates. If you give a song a "thumbs ups" — the way you tailor a station to your likes and dislikes — the service prompts you to tweet the track or post it on your wall. If you're listening to music on the mobile app and the band is playing a show nearby, it will alert you, and with a one click, you can share the info with a friend.

"We think of Earbits as an artist-centric radio platform," says CEO Joey Flores. "We're always looking for ways to connect a band with fans instead of just playing music for someone in the background. People are doing more on our website than just turning it on and tuning out."

And there's a good reason for this. On Earbits the songs themselves are commercials, which makes bands the customers, and of course, you — the listener — the product. Rather than encouraging users to click on ads and interact with brands, Flores hopes they'll discover bands, become fans, and buy their albums and concert tickets.

He desires this outcome for two reasons: For Earbits to make money, it must create enough value for a cash-strapped band to justify the expense and provide a return large enough that it demands reinvestment. If a band buys airtime to promote a show and converts a handful of listeners into concertgoers, they'll likely recoup their costs and use Earbits again. Flores also wants this to happen because as lifetime music fanatic, he believes that a world with more active fans (i.e. music buyers and concertgoers) could only be a better one.

"Don't just turn on the music and not wonder who it is," Flores laments. But wanting something to happen doesn't mean you can make it happen. The truth is that a majority of consumers aren't music fanatics and have no interest in doing a majority of these things. And, as Earbits has learned, even fanatics have limits.

Earbits has some of the most interesting sharing tools of any music service on their site. They spent lots of time building them only to find out that "like only 3% of people" will ever use the tools.

"Most people scroll right past [the Facebook toolbar]," Flores says, "they don't even see it."

This is illustrative. The very innovative feature that music and technology publications will praise Earbits for developing and having on their site ended up being the one fans didn't care to use.

Many music startups develop features in their products that they "think" fans want without actually testing them or embracing the hard truth that most fans may not want any of these things.

"We used to add a feature [to Earbits] and assume that it created more value [for users]," says Flores, referring the time period before his team read the influential book *The Lean Startup* by Eric Ries. Rather than making assumptions about the features users want and the value they create, they now utilize the "real metrics" that Ries advocates for, such as active users and user engagement, to determine if a feature is creating more value for their users and whether they should keep it. Flores says user engagement went down when Earbits added a search bar so that users could start a station by typing in an artist that they like, akin to what Pandora and rival services offer.

Before reading *The Lean Startup* and implementing its teachings, his company wouldn't have even been tracking that metric. "We would've just assumed that adding a search bar would've been a good thing," he says. "Actually, for some reason, it has a negative impact."

Flores says operating a startup for over a year without any real, important metrics and then embracing them wholeheartedly has "been really eye-opening." This sort of awakening is necessary for startups. Music elicits passion in people and some of them grow inspired to create products. These people are often fanatics who see problems to solve in their own lives and feel compelled to create solutions for everyone else. But fanatics aren't everyone else. Their wants and needs are different. A chasm exists between them and casual fans, and they don't see it.

Fanatics develop a product by making assumptions about what users want only to learn that most people don't have these problems and see no value in adopting their solution. As Ries argues in his book, a startup like this achieves failure by "successfully executing a plan that leads to nowhere."

This is the startup dilemma: A fanatic founder will often perceive a problem as being more universal than it actually is and mistakes his own experience as evidence that a solution should exist. Most people have never had such experiences and can't relate to the products they create.

A quick survey of the sector reveals that no one is doing quite what Earbits does. Services like Jango and Grooveshark let bands buy airtime and gain exposure, but do not encourage fans to attend their shows or share their songs. Pandora debuted a free concert series last year wherein it invited fans to attend a live performance by the rock band Dawes based on where fans live and the likelihood that they'd enjoy listening to their music. But it doesn't promote shows within its platform and doesn't allow artists to buy airtime.

Deli Radio, a newly launched music startup, enables fans to create radio stations that play music by bands that'll be playing shows nearby, the downside being that, since the service is free, bands can't geo-target fans.

Generally speaking, music services take a hands-off approach to promoting bands. "They're not making an effort to turn people into real consumers of those band's products," says Flores. "You're always trying to send them to McDonald's." Like broadcast radio before it, Pandora's customers are brands and it sells them a product: exposure to their audience. The music is the bait and there's nothing wrong with this. Many business models work like this.

Could Pandora make a better effort to help bands find fans? Of course. But here's the thing: It's not clear that casual listeners have a desire for this to happen. For them, a radio service that plays unfamiliar music and regularly alerts them about shows may be a bad experience. That's the reality. Flores is fighting a noble cause, and it's one worth fighting for. But he's targeting fanatics with Earbits and even they're pushing back against his efforts.

"At the end of the day, if you want to build a company that's good at promoting artists, you build a company that makes money from promoting artists," says Flores. It's a fair assessment.

But first Earbits must find fans that want bands promoted to them and it's a tough crowd.

February 21, 2012

MAINSTREAM FANATIC: SONGZA TAKES MUSIC PLAYLISTS TO THE MASSES

Every year, dozens of startups attempt the impossible: to make their product mainstream. In the music sector, this proves to be a particularly challenging task because startups are often founded by fanatics who are unlike the casual listeners they're targeting with their product.

The team at Songza, a music streaming service, faces this hurdle. The company presents itself as a destination for hand-crafted playlists and effortless music discovery, but the roll-out of its latest platform signals that its ambitions are much larger. Many companies have tried to create a mainstream playlist service before, but none have attempted this feat in the way that Songza has.

When a user visits Songza, they're now encouraged to use a feature that helps them select the perfect playlist for that time period. For example, if you open Songza on a Tuesday afternoon, it suggests you may be seeking music for "Working or Studying." If selected, it displays a list of genres, and if you pick "Pop," the playlists "The World of Adele" or "Soft Pop" are recommended.

This feature, branded as Music Concierge, is innovative and intuitive. It narrows the pool of playlists and eases the burden of picking one. By suggesting the right music for their day, it has the potential to increase the amount of enjoyment users derive from it, thereby enhancing their mood. But what's striking about the feature isn't what it does. The remarkable thing about Music Concierge lies in the fanatic activity that drives it and the effect it may have on those who use it.

Maximizing Music

There's a hoard of music experts and dedicated users behind Songza. These are the fanatics who swap songs in and out of the playlists for "Working or Studying," or "Getting Lucky," or "Unwinding After A Busy Weekend" until they achieve perfection.

They imagine themselves working or studying and attempt to align music with that experience in hopes that they can increase their focus and deepen their enjoyment of the task.

After several hours and possibly debates with friends, these fanatics arrive at a list of songs that suffice and now must determine how they fare in the real world. The next time they're working or studying, they'll cue up the playlist, make a few adjustments, and press play. Depending on how well the songs carry them through the designated activity, they'll either redo or finalize the playlist.

This process takes time and effort, more than a casual listener will devote. Songza removes this burden for casual users entirely and makes it easy to harvest the fruits of fanatic labor. It might just popularize the notion that different times of day call for different kinds of music if the service goes mainstream.

For decades, fanatics have had a romanticized idea about having a soundtrack to their lives. When they wake up in the morning, they dream of a playlist beginning that syncs up the perfect songs to their day and only pauses for dramatic moments between star-crossed lovers.

The introduction of the cassette opened the door to this music utopia, making it possible for fanatics everywhere to capture their favorite songs and blend them together in a thematic fashion.

But this form of playlist curation goes beyond that. Playing the right music at the right time is only one part of the equation. That's what a DJ does. When fanatics create playlists, they attempt to imagine future experiences and orchestrate music that maximizes the level of enjoyment they expect to derive from the activity alone. Their goal is to make the activity itself better through music.

Rather than settle for a playlist that's good enough, a fanatic explores all possible songs and chooses the best ones. This is a daunting task, but their playlists speak for themselves.

Songza has now packaged these playlists and made them accessible to casual listeners. The question is: Could a feature like Music Concierge produce negative effects? If so, what might they be?

Conveyer Belt

Products are conversations, and Songza mirrors what users tell it. We may not recognize the person staring back at us, but that reflection is us, and it speaks volumes about music fans today.

We're overloaded with choice, often opting to listen to the same old songs as a way to avoid facing unlimited options. Moreover, we outsource choice, using filters like iTunes and Pandora rather than "doing the work" ourselves. We stand alongside the conveyer belt that the web provides us, assigning thumbs up or down to songs as they pass us by. If unsure, we skip the song entirely because determining if we like it proves just as paralyzing.

Music in the digital age isn't always the paradise of choice we sought. As often, it's the paradox of choice. Recognizing this, Songza set out to develop a better product, one that helps users find great playlists and requires zero effort.

According to user feedback, even the act of typing in an artist name to create a playlist — the way a user creates a station on Pandora — demanded too much thought and energy. It also revealed that to them, the best music service is free to use with no strings attached or annoying audio ads. Added to this, Songza had to make it extremely clear to users how its product differed from web darlings like Pandora and Spotify, who are often wrongly compared to each other.

First the company released a new platform and a mobile app with an increased focus on its curated library of playlists and it has now placed Music Concierge at the forefront of that offering. This is significant because it encourages users to rely on a filter rather than on themselves and to pick a playlist over choosing one.

Perhaps more troubling than this result is the possibility that this passivity will carry over into the way users interact with the playlists they've chosen. Songza already assumes that a user is doing something else and listening to music, which diverts their attention from the response songs stir individually to the experience a playlist creates collectively. Rather than actively engaging with the music and the artists who create it, users begin an activity and use Songza to entertain them.

Now we shouldn't pretend that this scenario somehow differs from the way that most people listen to music. The distinction to make is that most musical experiences contain songs that have the potential to shake us from the motions of everyday life and captivate us to engage with them. When we listen to the perfect playlist for an activity, it never interrupts our workflow or demands attention.

Mainstream Fanatic

Generally, the first people a new music service attracts are fanatics. They instantly saw the value in joining Turntable.fm, the group listening service, and likely went on to become DJs. So too, they're the people who discover Songza and feel compelled to submit playlists for consideration.

The web platform and mobile app that Songza developed, though, required too much investment to cross the chasm and captivate a casual listener. To streamline the product and broaden its appeal, Songza introduced Music Concierge.

Turntable eluded the mainstream market and declined in use because it failed to translate the fanatic activities that drove its product into one that solved a problem that casual listeners have.

The wider narrative of Songza, however, goes much deeper. As the service gains traction, it will likely further the transition of music to merely the audio backdrop to our daily activities. It won't be assumed that we do something else and listen to music, it'll be accepted that we're always doing something else.

March 30, 2012

3 INSIGHTS INTO THE FUTURE OF GEOSOCIAL MUSIC

The geosocial revolution (see Foursquare and Facebook Places) promises to connect us to the places we visit and the people who frequent them, while helping us discover music in new ways, too. Over the past year, a number of startups have released location-based music apps, each aspiring to revolutionize the way we listen to music.

The most innovative of them, wahwah.fm, enables users to listen to music and simultaneously "broadcast" the session to a larger community. Meanwhile, other users can join the audience, and send messages back and forth in real-time. The app has the potential to give users a window into what music people are listening to nearby and what's trending in places far away. This is significant because it hints at how music culture and user habits may evolve.

Location has always limited our access to distant music scenes, and while the web has upended the tyranny of geography for some listeners, it remains an everyday constraint for most. As more music listening activities become linked to location — thanks to apps like wahwah.fm and others — it's clear that connected devices will continue to lower such barriers.

What happens next? Here are three insights into the future of geo-social music:

1. **Invisible culture emerges**.

A new layer of music culture is emerging all around us, built not from brick and mortar, but lines of code. It's located everywhere but because it's independent of place, it's situated nowhere.

Welcome to invisible culture, where music culture is not tied solely to places in the physical world, such as record stores or concert venues that can be reached by foot, but linked to locations through apps on connected devices. The digital revolution made our music and players invisible and weightless, and it has now made a layer of culture that's invisible and placeless.

When a user views this layer through a device, they'll be able to see a map of the area and the density of listener activity and music experiences linked to it. These can range from personal radio stations and group-listening rooms to user-tagged songs and photos, and maybe even the location of low-key artist events like jam sessions and house shows. Users will be able to move between digital and physical worlds, dropping by a local Turntable.fm room — either from the comfort of home or while out and about — and even request an invitation to attend a listening party that's being held at someone's place later that week.

On the one hand, the physical world is going digital, making it invisible. On the other, the digital world is becoming visible, making it physical. Music culture is everywhere, but situated nowhere.

2. **People are portals**.

Wahwah.fm often uses radio as a metaphor to describe what it does: Users listen to music and "broadcast" the session as a "radio station" that other users can "tune in" to.

That's not quite right. In science fiction, a portal is a magical or technological doorway that connects two distant locations separated by space-time. If you think about it, a portal is exactly what a person becomes when they air songs through wahwah.fm, as it opens up a doorway that enables faraway users to connect to another city's music scene and hear what people are listening to there.

This distinction is important because the connections being made through wahwah.fm are to people and not to places. Users can be connected wherever they are, whether at home or out of town, driving in a car or sitting in a coffee house.

Prior to the web, the music culture that formed in many places consisted of communities of people drawn together around physical locations such as record stores, clubs and radio stations whose social activities in the aggregate created a local scene. After a decade of disruption and consolidation brought forth by the digital revolution and other market forces, the scene-making activity at many of these locations has ceased, causing their attendant communities to fracture and move elsewhere.

More and more often, the new "where" for members of these communities is online. As smartphones made the web mobile and integrated with GPS, it provided developers with the platform needed to build geosocial apps that connect listening activity to individuals and enable communities to form around them. The person is becoming the portal — the primary hub of connectivity.

3. **Scenes become global**.

Since listening sessions in wahwah.fm are linked to your location, it means that user activity in New York or Los Angeles could be measured to reveal artists who are popular there. Those results could then be filtered to include only local artists, thereby creating a list of the most popular artists in that area. In this way, local scenes could be turned into a local music stations.

A wahwah.fm user who lives in New York could tap into Los Angeles and experience the sounds of the local scene, or perhaps enable a shuffle-like feature that would take him or her on a virtual tour of major scenes like Nashville, Atlanta, or Montreal, and highlight trending songs in those areas.

While a user listens to a song on this platform, they could be shown biographical bits about the artist, fan-captured photos from their latest live shows, and facts about the area to provide context.

Of course, listening to a scene isn't the same as being there. Roaming the streets of Los Angeles in Google Maps isn't the same as walking them. A scene is a place regarded as having a sound but it's the people and artists that shape it. What a listener hears then isn't the scene itself, but the musical essence of it.

That essence, though, gives users insight into scenes existing outside of their own. It also provides those of us without a local scene access to distant locations and the sounds attached to them. As people become portals, scenes will become global. Trending music will spread faster from one area to another, further influencing the sound artists produce and the music listeners hear.

The Future

This future may seem far out and in some ways it's already here. The web continues to teach us that the communities that form in the digital world eventually seep into the physical one.

Take Jelli, the social radio service, for example. Last year, a few broadcast radio stations in Las Vegas fully integrated Jelli into their offerings. This enabled a station's listeners to participate in a group chat and vote for songs in the service to be played on the air.

Over time, strangers became friends and regular users started hosting meetup groups around town where they used the digital service in a physical space. The radio station and the music it played gave them something to talk about, and soon people discovered they had other things in common.

"They came for the music and to get their song on the air, but they stayed because of the people they met in chat and the real-world meetups," says Jelli CEO Mike Dougherty. "These listeners are a great example of what a 'local scene' can be in the age of social media, mobile, and participatory media."

Indeed, the new music community is just that: a community. The culture and technology evolves, but human nature remains consistent. We're made to be together, and music catalyzes that impulse.

May 3, 2012

MUSIC DISCOVERY: THE PATH TO DIGITAL FAILURE

Billboard has doubled down on a particularly dangerous idea. In the trade publication's annual FutureSound white paper, it proclaims that music discovery is "The Key to Digital Fortune." This is, at best, egregious hyperbole and, at worst, completely mystifying. Senior correspondent Alex Pham, who wrote this section of the paper, concedes that enabling listeners to discover music is "much harder than it seems, as evidenced by the numerous efforts" and that such efforts have been largely fraught with "trial and error" for more than a decade. But Pham fails to question the promise of music discovery and why it's likely never to be fulfilled, let alone to address why music discovery is being championed as "the key to digital fortune" in the first place. It's clear that little thought went into the headline and that it has almost nothing to do with the reportage that follows, which is fine. But if the ostensible magazine of record wants to go out on a limb, it should notice that limb has already broken.

Music discovery is a dead pool of music startups, where zero successes exist. These startups die for a number of reasons, mainly steep royalties and licensing issues or the inability to convert a niche product into a sustainable business. If you look at the music startup sector, there are minuscule profits and fruitless exits. Shift your focus to the sole category of music discovery and things fare even worse. These services and apps register as blips on the radar of technology writers and receive launch coverage, only to fall back into obscurity and lie down to die. Some visualize related artists, while others suggest similar songs; none of them reaches a mainstream market. Few executives are so cynical that they will publicly guess how much runway a music startup has left (it's a very small world). But no one misses the chance to place a bet in private. Friends let friends found startups; no one wants to rock them to sleep. Even Pandora, the poster child for online music, is a spectacular failure whose days appear to be numbered.

The truth is that music discovery isn't a problem, and it's not a solution, either. Music listeners don't have trouble figuring out what to listen to; they simply don't know what to listen to next. They have more than enough music but not enough time to explore it. They enjoy re-listening to their favorite songs. Music startups believe that listeners like to discover music because the founding members love to discover music. In search of a killer solution, they reduce an organic and serendipitous process to a robotic and deliberate exchange. Arguably, the only stakeholders that have a "music discovery" problem are the artists whose music isn't being found. It's assumed that masking this problem as a product and shipping the resulting solution to music listeners works, but it hasn't. They still discover new songs they enjoy on broadcast radio and look up music videos on YouTube. *Billboard* says that music discovery creates "magical moments" that convert casual listeners to paying customers, but it never questions the demand for the trick or what it pays to be a magician. The only "magical" illusion that music startups have mastered to date is the vanishing act.

.

Music discovery requires a lot of work; no service can do that work for you. Sometimes, the right song falls into your lap at the right time and you manage to capture successfully it through a mobile app. You start listening to that song on repeat and become an uber fan of that artist. But if you want to discover music on a regular basis, i.e., more often than by chance, you must set aside a few hours to sift through and listen to a lot of "bad" music. This is the only reliable and tested method to "discover" great music. You can entrust a musicologist at Pandora or a disc jockey at Slacker to put in this effort and attempt to harvest the fruits of their labor, but no one can discover music for you. It doesn't matter what custom stations you create or how many "thumbs up" you dole out — your input determines Pandora's output. Slacker has 253 stations, but you, my friend, have six skips, and tapping a button isn't a "magical" moment that leads to fandom. There are dozens of equally flawed music discovery services that throw spaghetti against the wall in a similar fashion. These services help music listeners to stumble upon favorite songs and artists, but it still takes dedicated effort to find great music.

For over a decade, music discovery has revealed itself as a path to digital failure. A distressed sector of music startups has masked an artist problem and championed it as a consumer product, only to emerge broke and perplexed as to why casual listeners won't pay for their automated (and fanatic) solution. Maybe it's because "music discovery" isn't a problem they actually have, and if they did, it would take more than typing the name of their favorite artist into a website or handling over their entire Facebook "Like" history to solve. Maybe it's because "music discovery" takes so much work that no sane listener would ever be tricked into doing it unless, that is, they hear that their favorite torrent site is going to be shut down and they do some real research so that they "discover" what artists to type into the search box. It's crazy that we drone on and on about the perils of the "infinite search box" and "unlimited music choice," but we can't see that, if "music discovery" isn't a problem for pirate users, then it's not "the key to digital fortune" with legal consumers. Admit it: Music discovery is a lie that's never going to come true, and *Billboard* believing it's true won't make it true.

November 30, 2012

THE FUTURE OF MUSIC CHARTS

When you look at the *Billboard* charts, it's hard to find a focus. Since the major redesign of *Billboard.com* in 2009, few things have changed about the design of the charts, but numerous features have been added. You can share chart placements on major social channels and even play songs and buy downloads and tickets. There's also a dizzying array of info, from weeks spent on a given chart to artist news and non-*Billboard* chart activity. *Billboard's* charts now seemingly provide everything a music listener could ask for.

In recent years, *Billboard* has increased the number of charts it publishes, as well as their feature density. "Social 50" and "Uncharted," two tallies based on social media and music streaming, grew out of a partnership with data provider Next Big Sound. Months ago, the publisher also debuted an "On-Demand Songs" ranking, a joint effort with Nielsen and NARM. The downside of these new charts, however, is that they follow the same design and feature set as the rest: Aside from the artists and music that comprise each chart's entries, it's hard to tell them apart. And whether actual listeners get anything out of what are still primarily industry-facing charts is also an open question. Some are likely to provide better opportunities for music discovery than others, and some listeners will likely find a chart that suits their taste in music but the overall experience of reading *Billboard's* charts is underwhelming and mostly disappointing.

Some of the missing elements are context and interactivity. Below each chart entry, a cache of news items exists, but finding the correct story and reading the relevant bits is laborious. By the time you find the pieces you need to see the bigger picture (how a song charted and why it moved), you have likely left the website and abandoned the puzzle. The charts are also passive. Listeners can share to Twitter that "We Are Never Getting Back Together" by Taylor Swift is #1 on the Hot 100 chart but they have no means to register their opinion or impact that ranking.

There are reasons for such shortcomings. *Billboard's* charts are tied to an old platform. To enhance their style and functionality, the company would need to pay for another costly update and get a new partner for music streaming. Currently, *Billboard's* chart playback is dependent on Myspace, which does a good job but is still full of holes. Seeking direct licenses from the record labels is still cost-prohibitive, so that leaves the option of partnering with online music services like Spotify or Rdio to power playback.

Another huge dependency lies in data. A majority of the data for *Billboard's* charts currently comes from third parties (Nielsen and Next Big Sound), who primarily deliver information on a weekly basis. With this setup, empowering listeners to influence chart rankings wouldn't be much fun due to updates happening only once a week. And layering a Reddit-like voting system on top of the existing charts would again require a new platform, not to mention the challenge of implementing gaming mechanics and anti-gaming mechanisms.

Put simply, things are the way they are because they are. That's what the status quo is.

Better Widgets

Everyone is trying to create a better widget but that doesn't always translate to a better experience. Pandora and Spotify, the most popular online music services, enable listeners to click a play button. And while years of market research and user feedback have informed the location of that control and years of product development and technology advancement have allowed for seamless music playback, the experience ends as soon as it begins. You could argue that the music is the experience, and the fact that it plays every time you press that button should be considered a miracle (it is), but the "future" of music often feels unremarkable.

Certainly, the simplicity of Pandora is what makes it beautiful. There are hundreds of neat features that could be added but they would clutter the product and make it confusing. Spotify, on the other hand, contains sidebars laden with playlists, apps, friends, and activity. Features are crammed into every possible space. Most listeners who have used Spotify for a while encounter a highly personalized mess when they open the desktop app.

As regrettable as this may seem, this is what listeners want. It's not like they look at Pandora or Spotify after they click play anyway. Music is merely the audio backdrop to their daily activities. Nevertheless, we shouldn't accept widget after marginally improved widget as progress. There must be room to improve, if not rethink the experience.

Earbits, an Internet radio service, shows us the potential for a different approach. The player, inspired by thesixtyone, features a high-quality photo of the artist and a responsive interface. As you listen, you're prompted to join their mailing list, download their latest album, or like their Facebook page, among other things. You can also click to view photos, leave comments, and view their biography that includes discography, merchandise, and upcoming shows. When you give a "thumbs up" to a song you enjoy, you're given the option to tweet or share it.

The main reason this approach stands out is that Earbits markets music. An artist can submit their music to the service, and once approved, they can buy "airtime" to expose listeners to new songs or promote tour dates. The more listeners Earbits can drive to an artist's mailing list or downloads, the more money that artist will have (in theory) to invest in their online marketing efforts. So far, this trade-off seems to be working. According to Brian Hazard of Color Theory, who has successfully used Earbits several times now, "If you're willing to pay for text ads on Google or Facebook, you might as well get the plays thrown in at about the same price."

Most of the innovation in online music happens around emerging artists because the barrier to entry is lower and the licensing costs are lighter. If Earbits started out with mainstream popular music, it would enter a crowded market with established players and high overhead. Without a larger partner to provide distribution, the company would need to slog it out to build a user base and gain leverage. Years later, Earbits might earn enough clout to negotiate with the record labels for exclusive songs or artist participation, but the odds are against it. It would have a better widget tied to the same inventory. The experience would be immersive but nothing else about the service would be exclusive.

So why don't Pandora or Spotify become more music-focused like Earbits? For Pandora, the brands are the customer and the audience is the product. Promoting Frightened Rabbit's Facebook page over Miller Lite's radio station won't pay the bills. And there is also the argument that a majority of Pandora's users are passive listeners who likely don't want to be bothered with mailing lists and album-release prompts. Spotify, for its part, does promote music to some degree, but mostly through ads on the free version. It's a slippery slope, because if Spotify took cues from Earbits, it would be increasingly pressured by labels to offer more prompts. A developer could test similar features in a Spotify app, assuming that they were to comply with their strict guidelines. In the end, both companies want to create a better experience, but for now, we're stuck with pretty good widgets.

The Disruptors

The most innovative take on charts to date is We Are Hunted. The service indexes the most popular emerging songs online and presents them in a beautifully designed interface. Each placement on the tally can be shared to social channels, purchased through digital retailers, or used to create a playlist. One can also click to view an artist profile that features their latest news, tour dates, and biography. Mixed in with the tally are featured songs that can be downloaded for free in exchange for an email address. At its heart, however, We Are Hunted catalyzes music discovery more than it provides an authoritative chart.

Initially, publications heralded We Are Hunted as the "*Billboard* of the social web" because it gathered sentiment data from forward-thinking sources like blogs, social media, message boards, and P2P networks. No one had launched a social chart at the time, but Hunted isn't *Billboard*. It's a pretty list and no one knows what appearing on it means. The data isn't compiled directly from the sources and it's unclear what those sources are and how they're weighted. Unlike a *Billboard* chart, Hunted isn't transparent, quantified, or consistent. It's a playlist generator, not an industry currency. That's the point. Hunted is a filter, and much like KCRW or *Pitchfork*, it helps listeners to discover music. As such, Hunted may look like a chart but it's really a utility.

The next challenger to the *Billboard* throne arrived in 2010. BigChampagne, the media measurement company (since acquired by Live Nation), launched its Ultimate Chart. What separated the tally from the *Billboard* Hot 100 is that it measured the popularity of a song across a broader array of data sources, which included online music services and social platforms. At the time, *Billboard* primarily measured popularity by radio play and music sales. As a result, when an artist stopped being heavily rotated on radio and moving units, they would tumble on *Billboard's* Hot 100. But should this happen? After all, we know that spikes in activity come and go, but many artists continue to be popular online and off regardless. This is the oversight that BigChampagne sought out to correct with the Ultimate Chart. To some, this effort looked like more of the same. To others, it was a game-changer.

Shortly thereafter, MTV unveiled its artist-ranking service, Music Meter. Like We Are Hunted, the chart highlights up-and-coming artists and is based on sentiment data (provided by The Echo Nest), but it also tracks social buzz, music streams, and purchase metrics. As reporter Austin Carr at *Fast Company* aptly described it, "The chart is based on velocity rather than absolute popularity, so it will only show artists who are rising quickly — not those who are sitting in the No. 1 spot." To avoid the kind of criticism leveled at the Ultimate Chart (all pop, no surprises), MTV chose to strip out the most popular artists, like Lady Gaga and Justin Bieber, in an attempt to avoid comparison and create a music discovery experience. In recent months, MTV has removed the beta label from Music Meter and expanded the offering to include editorially determined categories like "Up & Coming," "Hip-Hop," and "Indie."

These are curious and ultimately compromising decisions. First off, chart rankings are generally determined by aggregated data, not personal opinions. Who decides which popular artists should be excluded? The Echo Nest does have metrics that take into account the "familiarity" and "hotness" of an artist, which likely help MTV to create a blacklist for Music Meter, but someone must be checking the chart for errors and removing outliers, too. Meanwhile, another instance of human meddling is in the genre distinctions. Again, The Echo Nest evaluates the sentiment surrounding an artist, and if a majority of the blog posts and news items refer to an artist as "indie," the categorization of indie by MTV is probably close, if not correct. But genres are an editorial distinction and "indie" is a very flimsy one at that. Music Meter is often called a chart, but MTV knows better. It's a discovery experience.

One Direction

Popular music is ripe for disruption. The reality is that two-thirds of younger listeners watch the videos for their favorite singles on YouTube and still experience Top 40 on traditional radio. A much smaller group listens to music on Pandora and Spotify, and a majority of them have likely never heard of Earbits, thesixtyone, or We Are Hunted. These listeners have only known a world of better widgets because no one has sought out to create a better experience. Even the mighty Google, which debuted its music service in 2011, has succumbed to the fate of attaching a play button to an otherwise underwhelming platform.

Consider this thought experiment. What if you created an online music service that offered free music streams subsidized by ticket and merchandise sales? What if the service tracked what you listened to and it provided you with suggestions on what concerts to attend and what band merchandise to buy?

For example, as you listened to "What Makes You Beautiful" by One Direction, you would be notified that they are playing three consecutive nights at the Staples Center in Los Angeles (where you live). If you wanted to, you could buy tickets for the show in a few clicks. Or, perhaps, as you start singing along to "We Are Never Getting Back Together" by Taylor Swift, you're presented with a few photos of her latest tee shirts.

It's difficult to say if sales from such a service could support the costs of running an online music service but the idea brings up an interesting point. There are many things that a casual listener of One Direction or Taylor Swift may want to know but never learns. For a million reasons, the news of a tour or new tee shirts never reaches them, nor does the release of a new single or album. Unless a listener becomes a fan of the artist on social platforms or signs up for the mailing list, it's likely that they'll never encounter most of the artist's updates.

As Earbits demonstrates, there are a number of ways that personal and relevant messages could be delivered to listeners through a music service. On Spotify, this is a huge and frequently missed opportunity. If you're a Green Day fan and have several of their albums starred, it's likely that Spotify never alerted you that their latest album, Uno!, was coming out. Unless you checked out the "What's New" section, you would have missed it.

Swarm.FM, a new music discovery app for Spotify, scans your library and recommends new releases based on your listening activity, favorite artists, and trending albums. It has other neat and helpful features, but this one is particularly enlightening. You will likely spot a new album by one of your favorite artists that you didn't know existed, which can be an embarrassing moment for any listener. In a way, scrolling through the Swarm.FM feed can feel disheartening because you can see a river of music that you've been missing out on and wish you had known about sooner. But it's comforting, too, because now the app will keep you up to date.

What would be better is if these songs were sewn into the experiences you already engage with. This is a simple service that traditional radio has provided for years, but gets lost online. When Lady Gaga debuts the first single from her upcoming album *Artpop*, stations will place the song next to familiar programing and enable you to discover it. All listeners have to do is continue to tune in and Ryan Seacrest will handle the rest.

Imagine that your thumb history on Pandora or library on Spotify served as a musical brain that powered custom stations and drove similar discovery. The latest songs from artists you love would automatically be rotated into the mix alongside other favorites. Radio has taught us that listeners need to be exposed to songs multiple times before they become familiar, and that this familiarity plays a strong role in how much they enjoy them. Songs don't grow on us but their pattern does. It becomes familiar and we like predicting it. For most listeners, pure music discovery isn't pleasurable or useful. They only want to hear new songs as the byproduct of a larger experience.

Future Charts

Charts are one of the largest missed opportunities in the music industry. They must move beyond a static tally of artists and music and become more interactive, making it so fans can impact the outcome. Charts must also make it easy for fans to understand why an artist appears on them by integrating stories into the tally. And most of all, charts must shift from a ranked order of the most popular artists and music that updates weekly to a real-time data utility that powers a broad array of experiences and enables discovery.

TastemakerX, a social music discovery game, hints at what real-time interactivity makes possible. It allows fans to "buy" shares of emerging artists that are growing in popularity and earn points for discovering them early. Over time, fans build a virtual portfolio of artists and compete to be recognized as influencers. To make TastemakerX reflect the real world, in real time, the company partnered with The Echo Nest. The game leverages their "dynamic music intelligence" to instantly price and track artists as shifts in their online popularity occur, which enhances the realism of the marketplace. The challenge, of course, is that TastemakerX isn't real. The entire experience happens in a silo and fans who play for keeps gain mere bragging rights. Such pitfalls haven't hindered the growth of fantasy sports, but they'll likely curtail the adoption of fantasy music.

Someday, there will be real-time, fan-powered charts. When that day comes, the moment a new song by Rihanna hits an inflection point of several million Spotify plays and YouTube views, it'll debut on the tally. Fans will be able to share that milestone with their friends through social platforms and even vote to help the song rise higher. In turn, they'll accumulate influence based on how the song fairs. A chart could, in theory, become a feedback loop that connects the artist and fan. So as Rihanna sees her song explode in popularity, she may gush to her fans and thank them for loving her song. She could even urge them to play and vote for the song more in an attempt to send it to #1. Fans could then share their small part of the larger story of her success.

Another music startup that provides a window into the future is CitySounds.fm. Launched in 2009 at Music Hack Day, the web app lets you listen to cities as radio stations. For example, if you click on New York or Los Angeles, you can hear the latest songs uploaded to SoundCloud by artists in that area. From there, you can also filter the station by popularity and genre. This app is compelling because it allows you to get a feel for different music scenes. "What we wanted to do first was tap into the vibe of each city. What music is popular right now, and where," said founder Henrik Berggren in an interview with *Evolver.fm*. "That was our intention."

That stated intention also reveals what becomes possible with geographical data. If you had behavioral data on the popularity of artists and songs in Los Angeles, it's likely that you could filter that set to those that are native to that area. And if you can develop a chart for Los Angeles, that means you could do Austin and Nashville, too. Fans would be able to play the top 25 indie bands in Seattle and then check out the #1 hip-hop act in Brooklyn. Starting out, every city in the U.S. would debut real-time, geo-based chart and later on, maybe scenes across the globe.

It stands to reason that an infrastructure like this would be capable of identifying when an artist from Los Angeles becomes popular among listeners in Minnesota, which may inform an artist's decision to route their tour in that direction. To bring this full circle, if this service also recommended tickets and merchandise, it would be able to alert listeners in the Twin Cities area that their favorite band will be stopping by in the coming months. And if you happen to end up being a fan standing in the front row at the Frightened Rabbit show, that's a pretty good experience.

October 18, 2012

BEATS MUSIC: CROWDED MARKET GAINS NEW RIVAL

Industry pundits and executives looked at the file-sharing and torrent downloading craze and saw millions of people who desired unlimited access to music but lacked a legal service to satisfy their needs. Stockpiles of MP3s and bloated iPods evidenced a potential market for an entirely new model where every song on iTunes could be streamed from the cloud for a monthly fee. This fantasy of a "celestial jukebox" has always appealed deeply to fanatic listeners who dreamed of Santa giving them the entire inventory of Amoeba Music for Christmas. But what about the mainstream market — the millions of casual listeners? Can this jukebox attract their interest?

To date, more than a decade into the digital revolution, no subscription music service has broken through to mass appeal. Spotify, a media darling and royalty scapegoat, boasts five million paid subscribers around the world, one million of which reside in the U.S. Rhapsody, the longest-running service, claims to stand above the one million mark, while newer entry Rdio, which has never shared numbers, is suspected to have far fewer subscribers. Meanwhile, Muve Music, a music plan bundled with Cricket Wireless phones, recently announced that it has surpassed 1.1 million subscribers since its early 2011 launch — more than any rival company in the U.S.

Beats Electronics, the creators of the high-end headphone brand, sees opportunity in the lack of any real subscription-model success to date. Since acquiring the fledgling music startup MOG in 2012, Beats has hired Ian Rogers from Topspin Media and positioned him at the helm of Beats Music. In tandem with this move, the company made a substantial investment in Topspin and named it a strategic partner that will supply photos, videos, and products from artists to the revamped MOG service. Both companies said that this collaboration stems from a "shared belief" that music services should "do a better job" at connecting fans to artists.

According to Bob Moczydlowsky, SVP of product and marketing at Topspin, music listeners should be able to find out when their favorite artist is performing nearby, be able to view an artist's Twitter feed, and see what products they have for sale, all while playing songs in a music service. Essentially, listeners should be able to dive as deeply as they wish into a newly discovered artist without having to leave to visit a site or start a Google search. Currently, listeners cannot navigate Taylor Swift's site or Facebook page from Pandora or Spotify. Such services are, in the words of Moczydlowsky, "a walled garden" where the apps are a mere "utility that delivers the sound."

For fanatic listeners, discovering a new artist opens a rabbit hole that leads to others. But before fanatics take that journey, they often want to learn everything they can about their initial find. With such listeners willing to engage, the fear is that current services do not give them enough to explore, which can hinder the discovery experience as well as the potential for them to be converted into consumers of an artist's products. Subscription services may have gotten better at making the actual music available as catalogs continue to grow but spreading the word to listeners about upcoming tours and releases remains an uphill battle.

The industry has long urged Spotify and Pandora to help artists to bridge this gap, and in recent months, the situation has improved. Pandora has revamped its web and mobile apps, making it easy for users to find lyrics, a short biography, and an overview of discography. Spotify, of course, allows users to play all of an artist's songs without limits but that is the main benefit to the otherwise limited offering. It has also enabled developers to create apps centered on artists and record labels for the platform, which is a huge step forward.

Rogers of Topspin and Trent Reznor, the industrial rock icon and newly appointed executive at Beats Music, have a much bigger vision. They will attempt to connect the artist layer to the music service. The thinking is that by integrating ticketing and merchandise sales directly into Beats Music, listeners will move through the marketing funnel more readily and convert at a higher rate. With credit cards already on file, such sales would be friction-free like Amazon or iTunes checkout, and lucrative for everyone involved. Such an arrangement would align Beats Music's business model more closely with artists and make it less dependent on advertising and subscriptions for revenue.

"The challenge of the funnel — be it the traditional sales funnel studied in business school, or one specific to digital music — is that moving people from each phase gets harder and harder based on transactional friction," says Jason Feinberg via email, VP of Digital Strategy at Epitaph Records, whose roster includes punk legends like Bad Religion, Social Distortion, and NOFX. "Fans have to be reached, made aware, made interested, given relevant options, and be able to easily and conveniently conduct a transaction." Combining all these elements into a music service, he says, could lead to "a noticeable increase in conversion."

How much money is on the table? Dave Kusek, a business consultant and former CEO of Berkleemusic.com, says there is "a complete disconnect between where most music is discovered today, and the $2.2 billion in annual merch revenue. The vast majority of merch is sold at the venerable merch table at any given concert." If merch distribution were aligned with the direction the online music market is heading, Kusek believes that it "would serve artists and merch companies extremely well, and potentially unlock a flood of new revenue." Added on top of this fair sum is the $2.34 billion in tickets sold to the Top 100 U.S. tours in 2011, according to *Pollstar*, a trade magazine.

More importantly, Beats Music could enable artists to take ownership of the fan relationship through every stage of the funnel, or at the very least, see inside the funnel and reach listeners for a small price. As Rogers has lamented in the past, the fatal mistake many artists make is they send fans to iTunes to buy music or Facebook to friend them and lose the opportunity to capture their email address for future contact. If artists do not collect and own this valuable dataset, they forfeit the ability to grow and monetize their audiences. Access to contact info and listening statistics in the Topspin dashboard would allow artists to more effectively target and market to Beats Music users.

Trusted Sources

The opportunity for Beats Music is to "create a trusted brand" in music, said Rogers on a conference call with various journalists and media outlets shortly after a flurry of news reports that he was taking the Beats Music job. He said part of that trust is listeners knowing they are going to receive high-quality, human-curated recommendations and not simply an infinite search box. Meanwhile, Reznor told the *New Yorker* in an interview that rather than relying solely on algorithms to power the music Beats Music suggests to listeners (if you like Taylor Swift, then you might like Sugarland) a network of music experts will point them down less traveled paths. So instead of the obvious fare, a country music aficionado may send listeners to Reba McEntire or Dixie Chicks.

Of course, the notion that music services need programming, as Beats Electronics CEO Jimmy Iovine put it, is not necessarily new. Rhapsody and eMusic employ editorial teams to write blog posts about the trending and popular music, and Slacker and Songza rely on professionals to seed their playlists with the freshest and hottest songs. So too, Rdio has developed social discovery features that enable users to follow tastemakers and receive updates about music they listen to or add to their collections.

Despite the number of programed services already available, the right formula for the "killer app" of discovery curation remains elusive. The problem is that listeners who like the notion of "millions of songs in your pocket" tend to be music fanatics with insatiable appetites and deep knowledge. They prefer to dig through record bins and program playlists themselves. They already have "trusted sources" like KCRW and Hype Machine who assist in exposing them to new artists. No one in the know about the latest music and apps is missing out or seeking a different solution. Spotify and Rdio work just fine for fanatics.

But Rogers and Reznor want to "take subscription music to the mainstream and really get it to scale." To accomplish this feat, Beats Music's staff needs to program the songs that casual listeners care most about hearing: the freshest, hottest songs by top-ranked artists. Such advice may sound rudimentary but Beats Music must develop a *Now That's What I Call Music* sensibility. The great irony of Spotify is that the songs that get played on Top 40 radio are exactly what casual listeners play there. Yet curation and discovery apps like Shuffler.fm and We Are

Hunted cater to fanatic listeners and mainly focus on surfacing songs that are trending in the music-geek blogosphere.

Why is this? Startup founders and app developers often succumb to a "fanatic fallacy" that leads them to believe casual listeners can be re-educated to like "good" music through the labor of sifting and searching for songs but they rarely convince anyone to put in such effort. So they resort to taking the work out of music discovery, often by hand-curating the most beloved songs on blogs or by aggregating them through various algorithms. The hope is that if it makes music discovery easier, casual listeners will teach themselves to like "good" music. What founders and developers come to find, though, is that casual listeners just don't care enough to make that investment.

"I believe that as an industry we put too much faith in music discovery," says Feinberg. "I have no doubt that there are many fans that do want to discover new music, but I find far more 'average users' (i.e. people not in our industry) that simply want to pick something they love and hit play." Listeners can tune into genre radio stations on Spotify and Pandora but these are often pigeonholes that range from vast tunnels to tiny cages that are either too generalized or too specific. Likewise, there is no way to fine-tune a station beyond rating songs with a "thumbs up" or "thumbs down," which can lead to listeners protecting the songs they already love (thumbs up) while dismissing the unfamiliar before really giving it a chance (thumbs down).

Many broadcast radio station lessons have not been applied to subscription services. 1) People want to listen to popular music and hear a few old favorites and new hits along the way, 2) The songs they discover should be from the best album releases by their favorite artists, and 3) The songs that listeners give "thumbs up" to on a station are likely the same songs that they want to hear in similar experiences. The best experience for casual listeners who love Nicki Minaj may be to recommend that they listen to Melanie Fiona and to seed her single "4AM" into a station, and if listeners favorite that song, alert them the next time a new single debuts.

Raw discovery, for example, listening to Hype Machine or We Are Hunted, is a bad experience for casual listeners. The songs are unfamiliar and eccentric. To make music discovery more accessible, it should be directly integrated into Beats Music. A listener's library should be the "musical brain" that powers the experience, shuffling in old favorites and next hits. It should be the central location where the songs a listener has collected from the physical and digital worlds are and where disparate online identities are seamlessly unified. It should be a map that guides them, enhancing activities and brightening moods without needing to be "seeded" with artists or songs to grow.

"In order to succeed, Beats Music would need to be designed largely for casual listeners, because fanatics are by their very nature the rarer creature," says Aaron Tap, a musician who is best known for playing guitar with Matt Nathanson and Paula Kelley. "The big question hanging over every music service is what really does the average listener want?" The answer, according to Rogers, is "curation by trusted sources," which he calls "the next phase of internet distribution." On this point, Tap agrees, adding that there is "not much personality" in current services, and a well-curated one, along the lines of Jack FM or KCRW, "could be all things to all people."

This is why Rogers and Reznor cannot just strive to make Beats Music a "better" Spotify with a simpler design and stronger curation. The truth is that Rdio has already created a better Spotify, and Slacker Radio has always been a better Pandora. iHeartRadio sits somewhere in the middle, with a combination of broadcast radio and custom stations, and Songza and 8tracks probably tie for having the best curated playlists. YouTube and Vevo, the largest services, display music videos, which continue to be the most popular media among younger listeners. Not one does a great job at curating and surfacing old favorites and new hits, i.e. the songs that casual listeners want to hear.

Pieces Together

Billboard writer Glenn Peoples says that subscription services have not reached a wider market because they are not "built, packaged, and priced" for mainstream listeners. The leading services like Spotify, Rhapsody, and Rdio are for fanatic listeners who will "invest a great deal of time and money in the product." Peoples argues that such services "need to become easier to use and a better value for the price." Aping iTunes may have been the best way for rival companies to translate the idea of unlimited music for their listeners, the Iovine pitch goes, but Beats Music will take a different approach, possibly bundling the service with mobile devices and pricing the plan very low.

During a Twitter exchange, professor and researcher David Touve suggested that the price of music services should "match the nature of demand" of $5 a month rather than the industry standard of $10 because casual listeners only spend less than $60 a year on music. Rhapsody recently introduced a new plan with MetroPCS that dropped rates to $5 a month, proving that such a price is possible. But whether it can help Rhapsody convert and retain subscribers is the big question. The greater problem is that making subscription services cheaper to buy and easier to use will not magically enthuse apathetic casual listeners.

"The idea of being able to hear anything they want, whenever they want, appeals to the mass market — but it's not actually what most want in practice," says Jason Herskowitz, who contributes to Tomahawk, a cross-platform music player. "I think what they want is a few giant play buttons that just play them stuff they love . . . with the majority of it being stuff they already know they love with a few prospects of new love sprinkled in between." Entrepreneur Bruce Warila summed up this concept perfectly, saying casual listeners want a "fader" that calibrates "more to less of the music I already love and less to more of new tracks you think I love."

The music industry has bought into this idea that casual listeners are fanatic listeners with less time. If we just make it easier for them to harvest the fruits of fanatic labor they will love the same music. In effect, the "programmer" needed for music services is a fanatic listener that takes them on a guided tour of their rabbit holes. Casual listeners, in this context, are viewed as lazier or older listeners (often both). With more ambition or time, they too would research and discover new music but the effort is too great. Rather than accept that casual listeners are different listeners, we have wrongly labeled them as "lesser" listeners.

But casual listeners never shopped at record stores and sought advice from the clerks. They walked into big box retailers like Wal-Mart or Best Buy where the staff is mostly clueless about giving informed advice about music, and grabbed the album with the single they liked off an end-cap. Casual listeners do not spend their free time researching on music blogs and programming playlists. They turn on KIIS FM in their car and Ryan Seacrest introduces the next Justin Bieber or Rihanna single. They have seen Nickelback perform live twice and eagerly captured Instagram photos of singer Chad Kroeger dousing the entire front section with Bud Light. The "soundtrack" to their life is "Bartender Song" by Rehab.

To be clear, even casual listeners are "fanatic" about some artist or band. They might discover One Direction and grow so passionate that they read the latest gossip, print out and hang up pictures, and share lyrics on Facebook and Twitter. They might even become so committed that they lash out against "enemies" in online feuds. But it is their orientation toward culture more broadly that is different. They will not also become passionate about activities like discovering songs on blogs or listening to records. A fanatic of this sort is someone that you are, not someone you become. Fanaticism toward music has never been the destiny that pundits have made it out to be.

In a presentation in 2006, Rogers accused iTunes of being "a spreadsheet that plays music," adding in a recent blog post that subscription services have yet to find "a way to surround music with context." The crux of his claim is that listening to music used to consist of physical media which was the object that produced brilliant sound, and the ever-important artwork and album booklet that, taken together, formed a cohesive experience. When fanatic listeners bought an album and played the songs, they pored over the photos and lyrics inside. To see the faces of their heroes and read their words (maybe for the first time) gave the music additional meaning.

Rogers (of course) is not the only voice in this choir. Speaking of a recent redesign, Rdio VP of product Malthe Sigurdsson said the company's new web and desktop apps transform "the boring, spreadsheet-like way of consuming digital music into something visual and dynamic." The word choice here is very specific and revealing. It is tempting to argue that listening to music should be emotional and engaging but that is also a fanatic fallacy. Casual listeners often want music to be anything but those things. They are way too busy working and studying. The problem with Turntable.fm, after all, is that fanatic listeners love the experience but stop getting anything done and leave.

This is not to say that improvement to existing music services is not needed, or that it should not be attempted. Rogers and Renzor have good reason to deem the state of online music unacceptable and to challenge the status quo (they both share a well-documented history of doing the latter — sometimes even together. The future they hoped for and the present they occupy are vastly different. It's a music utopia that is neither lost or found. The web did not create a middle-class of musicians and "1,000 True Fans" to support each of them. Rather it gave us a relatively successful handful of artists who did all right, and many more who did not, and an upper class that largely continues to control tours and charts.

After years of fighting with record labels and downloading millions of songs, music listeners have been given the "celestial jukebox" that at least some of them always fantasized about. They can pull out their computer and have unlimited access to music on Spotify or Rdio for free. Hell, Amoeba Music has even made much of its brick-and-mortar store available for sale online. Everything is amazing and most listeners are either blissfully ignorant or very happy. Mainstream or not, the "promised land" already exists, and it would seem worth asking, as actor Jack Nicholson once did, "What if this is as good as it gets?" Perhaps we'll find out later this year, after Beats Music launches.

February 12, 2013

EPILOGUE

It would take a long time to reflect on what I got right or wrong in the essays in this book. Every day the music industry changes and evolves, and I grow and develop as a person. Many of the music startups mentioned have been acquired or shut down, and most of the industry experts quoted have been promoted or switched companies. Rather than lean backward and reflect on the past or lean forward and predict the future, I want to talk about the present state of music and technology journalism. There aren't many young writers with big ideas and new perspectives adding to the conversation about the future of music.

For many reasons, this isn't surprising because there aren't open jobs or big checks, and writing is extremely hard. But in other ways, it makes no sense because the music industry dream is alive and well. There are thousands of students enrolled in music industry programs around the world, and many more who are majoring in something that family and friends approve of, but still hold onto the hope that they will work in music when they graduate. So why don't these people speak up and let their voices be heard? Are they waiting for the permission that never comes or are they afraid that they will say something stupid?

I suspect that it's both of these reasons, among others, so let me give you some words of encouragement: no one else has had your personal experience of listening to and discovering music, nor have they seen how specific technologies have changed them over time. I want you to think about that for a couple days; start to take down notes, look for patterns or themes, and develop a theory. Next, I want you to talk to your friends and family about how they listen to and discover music; ask several objective questions and probe for deeper answers. What did you learn? What was your favorite story? Did you see any trends in your collected data?

If you spend some time on this exercise, I promise that you will learn something new and gain an insight interesting enough to write about. You have to understand that trade journalists and industry experts don't live in the real world and they certainly don't live in your world. They live in a bubble and oftentimes the air ran out a long time ago. They speak from their personal experience or recent statistics, but the truth is that no one has the total picture of the entire world.

For example, the coffee shop that I have been writing in at Fargo, North Dakota, is full of college students, young professionals, and older adults. I don't know if they use YouTube, Pandora, or Spotify, or if they have moved onto a new service that I've never heard of. Maybe they still listen to local radio and buy CDs at Target. How am I supposed to know? I'm an industry expert and user researcher, and you might think it's my job to know, but that's the opportunity that I'm trying to present to you.

There is no way that you are going to become an industry expert until you've become a student of the business for several years and been blessed with the opportunity to study under people smarter than you. It has taken me six years, two internships, two stints at Target, and three jobs to write these essays and build a body of work good enough to call this a book, and feel proud of the words that you are reading. I can only hope that my hard work will create more luck. But I wanted to stop the roller coaster of work and life to repeat my lesson: take an interest in people and be curious about their listening habits. Ask them questions and learn about their world. If they don't care about music as much as you do or say things that aren't novel and surprising, then you're talking to the wrong people.

I'm sure many of my friends and colleagues would argue that the music industry is in desperate need of people who understand it and have a sense of its history, but please don't wait until you've gained expertise before you share your perspective. I started this journey as a 20-year-old college student and label intern, and have become a 26-year-old industry expert and user researcher.

If you need permission, here you go: become a people expert and raise your voice today.

ACKNOWLEDGMENTS

I would like to thank Gordan Tweit, who read my lyrics and encouraged me to write more. You believed in my dreams. I would like to thank Scott LeGere, who inspired me in class and exposed me to big ideas. You sent me down this rabbit hole. I would like to thank Bruce Houghton, who found my second blog post on the web and re-published it on *Hypebot.com*. You opened the door. I would like to thank Eric Garland, who joined me during my professional journey and led the way to the next adventure. We jumped through the window. I would like to thank Annie Licata, who cleaned up my earlier writing and edited the entire book. You made this project possible. I would like to thank Derek Pinnick, who read through the final edit and emboldened me to take my book to a publisher. You helped me to carry this project the last mile. Of course, I would like to thank my mom and dad, who have cared supported me through my life and career. I love you both.

CONTACT

Email: kyle.bylin@gmail.com

41715268R00102